HBR Guide to
Project
Management

Harvard Business Review Guides

Arm yourself with the advice you need to succeed on the job, from the most trusted brand in business. Packed with how-to essentials from leading experts, the HBR Guides provide smart answers to your most pressing work challenges.

The titles include:

HBR Guide to Better Business Writing

HBR Guide to Finance Basics for Managers

HBR Guide to Getting the Mentoring You Need

HBR Guide to Getting the Right Job

HBR Guide to Getting the Right Work Done

HBR Guide to Giving Effective Feedback

HBR Guide to Making Every Meeting Matter

HBR Guide to Managing Stress at Work

HBR Guide to Managing Up and Across

HBR Guide to Persuasive Presentations

HBR Guide to Project Management

HBR Guide to
Project
Management

HARVARD BUSINESS REVIEW PRESS

Boston, Massachusetts

Library of Congress Cataloging-in-Publication Data

HBR's guide to project management.
 p. cm.
 ISBN 978-1-4221-8729-6 (alk. paper)
 1. Project management. I. Harvard business review. II. Title: Guide to project management.
 HD69.P75H394 2013
 658.4′04—dc23

                2012026957

What You'll Learn

You've been asked to lead a project. You appreciate the vote of confidence, but are you panicking because you haven't a clue where to begin? Do you worry that stakeholders will tug you in a million directions, making it impossible to set clear goals, let alone deliver the goods on time and on budget? How will you know when to stick to your original plan and when to be flexible? And how will you keep all your team members excited about this project—when they have so many other pressures on them?

This guide will give you the confidence and tools you need to manage projects effectively. You'll get better at:

- Choosing the right team and keeping it humming

- Avoiding "scope creep"

- Zeroing in on critical tasks and mapping out a logical sequence

- Making heads or tails of Gantt and PERT charts

- Getting disruptive team members on board

- Keeping stakeholders in the loop

- Gauging your project's success

- Deciding when to cut bait

- Capturing—and using—lessons learned

Contents

Phase 3: IMPLEMENTATION

Contents

Phase 4: CLOSEOUT

Overview

Chapter 1
The Four Phases of Project Management

Whether you're in charge of developing a website, design-ing a car, moving a department to a new facility, updating an information system, or just about any other project (large or small), you'll go through the same four phases: planning, build-up, implementation, and closeout. Even though the phases have distinct qualities, they overlap. For example, you'll typically begin planning with a ball-park budget figure and an estimated completion date. Once you're in the build-up and implementation phases, you'll define and begin to execute the details of the proj-ect plan. That will give you new information, so you'll re-vise your budget and end date—in other words, do more planning—according to your clearer understanding of the big picture.

Adapted from *Pocket Mentor: Managing Projects* (product #1878), Harvard Business Review Press, 2006

Here's a chart that outlines the activities of each phase, plus the skills and tools you may need for doing the work:

PROJECT PHASES

Planning	Build-up	Implementation	Closeout
ACTIVITIES			
Determine the real problem to solve	Assemble your team	Monitor and control process and budget	Evaluate project performance
Identify stakeholders	Plan assignments	Report progress	Close the project
Define project objectives	Create the schedule	Hold weekly team meetings	Debrief with the team
Determine scope, resources, and major tasks	Hold a kickoff meeting	Manage problems	Develop a post-evaluation report
Prepare for tradeoffs	Develop a budget		
KEY SKILLS			
Task analysis	Process analysis	Supervising	Follow-through
Planning	Team building	Leading and motivating	Planning
Cost-benefit analysis of options	Delegating	Communication	Communication
	Negotiating	Conflict management	
	Recruiting and hiring	Problem solving	
	Communication		
TOOLS			
Work Breakdown Structure	Scheduling tools (CPM, PERT, Gantt)		Post-evaluation report: analysis and lessons learned

Planning: How to Map Out a Project

When people think of project planning, their minds tend to jump immediately to scheduling—but you won't even get to that part until the build-up phase. Planning is really about defining fundamentals: what problem needs solving, who will be involved, and what will be done.

Determine the real problem to solve

Before you begin, take time to pinpoint what issue the project is actually supposed to fix. It's not always obvious.

Say the CIO at your company has asked you, an IT manager, to develop a new database and data entry system. You may be eager to jump right into the project to tackle problems you have struggled with firsthand. But will that solve the *company's* problem? To increase the project's chances of success, you must look beyond the symptoms you have observed—*"We can't get the data out fast enough"* and *"I have to sift through four different reports just to compile an update on my clients' recent activity"*—to find the underlying issues the organization is trying to address. Before designing the database, you should ask what type of data is required, what will be done with it, how soon a fix is needed, and so on. If you don't, you'll run the risk of wasting time and money by creating a solution that is too simplistic, too complicated, or too late—or one that doesn't do what users need it to do.

Identify the stakeholders

The real problem will become even clearer once you figure out who all your **stakeholders** are—that is, which functions or people might be affected by the project's activities or outcomes, who will contribute resources (people, space, time, tools, and money), and who will use and benefit from the project's output. They will work with you to spell out exactly what success on the project means. Have them sign off on what they expect at the end of the project and what they are willing to contribute to it. And if the stakeholders change midstream, be prepared not only to respond to the new players but also to include all the others in any decision to redirect the project.

Whether you're managing a project in a corporation or working as an independent consultant, it's critical to have the support of the people you're working for. They may take a blue-sky view and demand an enormous amount of work within an unrealistic time period or expect you to perform miracles with inadequate resources or staffing. As the project manager, you'll need to make sure the requirements and resources line up fairly evenly, or you will set yourself up for failure.

Define project objectives

One of your most challenging planning tasks is to meld stakeholders' various expectations into a coherent and manageable set of goals. The project's success will be measured by how well you meet those goals. The more explicitly you state them at the outset, the less disagreement you will face later about whether you have met expectations. In the planning phase, however, much is still in flux, so you'll revise your objectives later on, as you gather information about what you need to achieve.

When defining objectives, think SMART. They should be:

- Specific

- Measurable

- Action-oriented

- Realistic

- Time-limited

Suppose your HR department has been tasked with identifying potential new providers for your company's health benefits plan because the current ones aren't delivering the level of service they should given how much money employees have to pay for them. The project's SMART objectives may be to:

1. **Survey** *<action-oriented>* at least **six** *<measurable>* providers that meet the department's minimum threshold criteria for service quality.

2. **Recommend** *<action-oriented>*, at the **June** *<time-limited>* board of directors' meeting, the **three** *<specific>* that offer the best and broadest coverage at a cost that is at least **10%** *<realistic>* less than the company's current per-employee contribution.

Keep the following factors in mind as you define your project's objectives:

- **Quality.** Identify quality standards, and determine how to measure and satisfy them.

- **Organization.** Calibrate goals depending on the people and other resources you have available.

- **Communication.** Determine what information each stakeholder needs and how to deliver it.

Determine scope, resources, and major tasks

Many projects fail either because they bite off more than they can chew and thus grossly underestimate time and money or because a significant part of the work has been overlooked. One tool that can help you avoid these problems is the **Work Breakdown Structure (WBS),** which aids in the process of determining scope and tasks and developing estimates. (See the sample later in this chapter.) The underlying concept is to subdivide complex activities into their most manageable units.

To create a WBS:

- Ask, "What will have to be done in order to accomplish X?"

- Continue to ask this question until your answer is broken down into tasks that cannot be subdivided further.

- Estimate how long it will take to complete these tasks and how much they will cost in terms of dollars and person-hours.

A WBS typically consists of three to six levels of subdivided activities. The more complex the project, the more levels it will have. As a general rule, you shouldn't have more than 20—and only an enormous project would require that many.

Here in the planning phase, don't worry about the sequence of activities. You will take care of scheduling in the build-up phase. Rather, use the WBS to create the framework that you'll fill in once you have a better sense of your staff, budget, and time constraints. Padding estimates is an acceptable way to reduce risk, but do it openly and communicate your reasons to the stakeholders.

As a result of your thoughtful planning, you'll be able to rough out an estimate of how many people—with what skills—you'll need for the project. You'll also have a good idea of how long the project will take.

Prepare for trade-offs

Time, cost, and quality are the three related variables that typically dictate what you can achieve.

$$Quality = Time + Cost$$

Change any of these variables, and you change your outcome. Of course, such alterations often occur in the middle of a project. If your time frame for developing a new database management system is suddenly cut in half, for instance, you will need to either employ twice the number of people or be satisfied with a system that isn't as robust as originally planned. Don't let bells and whistles get in the way of mission-critical activities. The key is to establish a level of quality that meets your stakeholders' needs.

Knowing from the start which variable is most important to each stakeholder will help you make the right changes along the way. It's your responsibility to keep everyone informed of any tweaks and tell them what the consequences will be in terms of time, cost, and quality.

WORK BREAKDOWN STRUCTURE

Sample Planning Document

Develop a Work Breakdown Structure (WBS) to ensure that you do not overlook a significant part of a complex activity or underestimate the time and money needed to complete the work. Use multiple pages as needed.

DESCRIBE THE OVERALL PROJECT:

The overall project will migrate 3 Web servers and databases to a new physical data center. The project requires that 5 new servers be provisioned in the new data center: these servers will mirror the production servers existing in the old data center. The new servers will be built to the same specifications as the old ones; they will run the same application and have the same content. Once implemented, the new equipment will be tested to confirm functionality. The sites will have a cutover and "go live" date. Finally, the old equipment will be decommissioned and reabsorbed into inventory.

MAJOR TASK

Obtain equipment.

Level 1 Sub Tasks

Purchase 3 Web servers and 2 databases.

Ship equipment to new data center.

Level 2 Sub Tasks

Cut P.O. and order servers.

Alert data center that equipment is slated for arrival.

Sub Task Duration

7 days

MAJOR TASK

Provision and implement equipment.

Level 1 Sub Tasks

Physically install hardware.

Load operating systems.

Load applications.

Mirror content to new servers.

Level 2 Sub Tasks

Rack and cable new equipment in data center and ensure physical and network connectivity.

Load base-level operating systems for Web and database servers.

Load application level software, including Web server software, database applications, and any required dependencies.

Copy configurations from production sites, transfer to new servers, and load appropriately.

Sub Task Duration

8 days

MAJOR TASK

Test equipment.

Level 1 Sub Tasks

Test machines.

Level 2 Sub Tasks

Ensure network connectivity, as well as Web and database access functionality and integrity.

Sub Task Duration

2 days

MAJOR TASK

Go live with new equipment.

Level 1 Sub Tasks

Cutover to new production site.

Data and content integrity check.

(continued)

████████████████████████████████████

MAJOR TASK (CONTINUED)

Level 2 Sub Tasks

Switch Web and database access to new sites.

Run a series of predetermined tests to ensure that data is accurate and that any updates since mirroring have been captured and applied as necessary.

Sub Task Duration

2 days

MAJOR TASK

Test again.

Level 1 Sub Tasks

Let sites burn in for 24 hours and check integrity once again.

Level 2 Sub Tasks

Run series of tests once more to ensure that updates and logging are functioning correctly.

Sub Task Duration

1 day

MAJOR TASK

Decommission old equipment.

Level 1 Sub Tasks

Remove equipment from data center.

Reabsorb equipment for future use.

Level 2 Sub Tasks

De-install equipment; erase software and content.

Ship equipment back to inventory.

Sub Task Duration

2 days

Build-Up:
How to Get the Project Going

In the build-up phase, you bring your team together. Time estimates become schedules. Cost estimates become budgets. You gather your resources. You get commitments, and you make them.

Assemble your team

Your first task in this phase is to assess the skills needed for the project so you can get the right people on board. This assessment flows directly from the Work Breakdown Structure you did during the planning phase, in which you developed your best estimate of the necessary tasks and activities. You may need to bring in people—either temporary workers or employees from other parts of the organization—who have certain skills. Don't forget to budget time and money for training to cover any gaps you can't fill with people who are already up to speed.

Plan assignments

If you've built your own team, you've probably already decided who will do what. Or, if you've inherited a team but worked with the members before, you can still make the assignments yourself. But if a new, unfamiliar group is assigned to you, list the people on the team, list the skills required, and talk to each team member about her own skill set before you match people to tasks. This approach starts the process of team communication and cohesion. For example, if the project calls for a skill no one on the team possesses, members may know someone else who has it—or they may express interest in being trained themselves.

Clearly, you can't do everything yourself, even if you want to. After you've decided how you will assign tasks to team members, give each person the information and resources needed to succeed—and then back off and let your team members do their jobs. You may, as the project proceeds, have to delegate more tasks than originally anticipated. Be flexible enough to do so—without forgetting that you, as project manager, are the one who's accountable for results. (See the sidebar "Tips for Delegating Effectively.)

Create the schedule

It would be nice if you could tally up the to-dos and say, "With the resources we have, we will need this much time"—and then get exactly what you've asked for. But the reality is, most projects come with fixed beginning and end dates, regardless of available resources.

To create a realistic schedule within those constraints, work backward from any drop-dead deadlines you know about—that is, dates that cannot be changed—to see when your deliverables must be ready. For instance, if an annual report is due for a shareholder's meeting and you know it takes the printer two weeks, then all the final art and copy for the report must be ready to go to the printer two weeks before the meeting.

Depending on the complexity of your project, you may also rely on tools such as the **Critical Path Method** and a **Performance Evaluation and Review Technique (PERT) chart** to help with the sequencing of tasks and a **Gantt chart** to map out their chronological order and duration. You'll learn how to use these tools elsewhere in this guide. For now, though, keep in mind the "working backward" rule of thumb and these basic steps for scheduling:

1. Use the Work Breakdown Structure or a similar outline to develop a list of activities or tasks, and

TIPS FOR DELEGATING EFFECTIVELY

- Recognize the capabilities of your team members.

- Trust your team's ability to get the job done.

- Focus on results, and let go of your need to get involved in how tasks are accomplished.

- Consider delegation as a way to develop the skills of your team.

- Always delegate to the lowest possible level to make the best use of staff resources.

- Explain assignments clearly and provide resources needed for successful completion.

- Deflect reverse delegation. Do not automatically solve problems or make decisions for your staff members. Focus on generating alternatives together.

plot out their sequence by determining which ones are critical to achieving the desired final outcome.

2. Assign each task a deliverable—for instance, "compose rough draft of survey questions."

3. Use deliverables to create a schedule with realistic due dates.

4. Identify bottlenecks that could upset the schedule.

5. Determine ways to remove bottlenecks, or build in extra time to get around them.

6. Establish control and communication systems for updating and revising the schedule.

7. Keep all stakeholders involved in and informed of the project's progress and any schedule modifications.

Hold a kickoff meeting

As soon as you've chosen your players and set the schedule, bring everyone together for a kickoff meeting. Go over the project's plan and objectives with the group in as much detail as possible, and review the proposed time frame. Be sure to clarify roles and responsibilities.

Encourage people to point out spots where problems may occur and where improvements could be made. Take all suggestions seriously—especially in areas where the team members have more experience than you do—and adjust your estimates and activities accordingly.

Develop a budget

The first question to ask when developing a budget is, "What will it take to actually do the work?" To determine your costs, break down the project into the following categories:

- **Personnel.** Have you included all costs, both ongoing and extra, for employees and contract workers? (This is typically the largest part of a budget.)

- **Travel.** Is everyone onsite, or will employees be brought in from other locations?

- **Training.** Does everyone know how to use all the necessary equipment and software? Do the members of your team possess all the required skills? Will training involve travel? Will you need to teach users how to implement your project when it's completed?

- **Supplies.** Will your team need anything in addition to the usual computers, software, and so on?

- **Space.** Do people have to be relocated? How much room will be required in the new space, and at what cost? Will there be ongoing maintenance expenses?

- **Research.** Will you have to buy studies or data to support this project? How much research will your team have to perform itself? At what cost?

- **Capital expenditures.** What expensive equipment or technical upgrades will be necessary to do the

job? Will any capital expenditures pay for themselves? If so, how?

- **Overhead.** What is your projected overhead expense? Is it in line with your company's standard
overhead percentage?

After you've entered the figures from these standard
categories into the budget, ask a trusted adviser what
you forgot. Did you overlook insurance? Licensing fees?
Costs for legal or accounting support?

A budget, no matter how carefully planned, is just
your best guess. Expect actual numbers to deviate from
original estimates, and stay as flexible as possible within
your limitations of time, quality demands, and total
money available.

Implementation: How to Execute the Project

It's time to put the plan into action. The implementation
phase is often the most gratifying, because work actually
gets done, but it can also be the most frustrating. The details can be tedious and, at times, overwhelming.

Monitor and control process and budget

Whether you have a formal project control system in place
or you do your own regular check-ups, try to maintain
a big-picture perspective so that you don't become en-
gulfed by details and petty problems. Project-monitoring
software systems can help you measure your progress.
No single approach works for all projects. A system that's
right for a large project can easily swamp a small one

with paperwork, whereas a system that works for small projects won't have enough muscle for a big one.

Respond quickly to changes in data or information as they come in, and look for early signs of problems so you can initiate corrective action. Otherwise, all you are doing is monitoring, not exercising control. Make it clear to your team that your responses to problems that arise won't do any good if you don't receive timely information. (In most cases, the weekly updates are fine.) But don't jump in to fix things too quickly—allow your team members to work out small problems on their own.

Watch the real numbers as they roll in to ensure that they are matching the budgeted amounts. Be ready to explain why extra costs are unavoidable. Common ones that sneak up on projects include increased overtime to keep things on schedule, consultant fees to resolve unforeseen problems, and fluctuations in currency exchange rates.

Report progress

Stakeholders will generally want regular updates and status reports. Consult with them to see how much information they'd like and in what format. Don't hide or downplay problems as they come up, or you can easily transform them into crises. If you keep your stakeholders informed, they may turn out to be good resources when issues do arise.

Hold weekly team meetings

When you're immersed in project details, it's easy to be diverted from critical activities to side paths that waste time. You and your team can stay focused by meeting

TIPS ON CONTROLLING PROJECT SLOWDOWNS

Try these approaches before accepting the inevitability of a delay in project completion:

- *Renegotiate with stakeholders.* Discuss the possibility of increasing the budget or extending the deadline.

- *Use later steps to recover.* Reexamine budgets and schedules to see if you can make up the time elsewhere.

- *Narrow the project's scope.* Can nonessential elements of the project be dropped to reduce costs and save time?

- *Deploy more resources.* Can you put more people or machines to work? Weigh the costs against the importance of the deadline.

once a week and periodically asking yourselves what's essential to the project's success.

Set clear agendas for your meetings. Try structuring them around production numbers, revenue goals, or whatever other metrics you've chosen to gauge performance. Many of your agenda items will naturally stem from targets the project has missed, met, or exceeded: For instance, you may need to discuss as a group whether to incorporate more travel into the project because you've

- **Accept substitution.** Can you go with a less expensive or more readily available item?

- **Seek alternative sources.** Can you get the missing item elsewhere?

- **Accept partial delivery.** Can you keep work going if you take the items that are ready now and receive the rest of the delivery later?

- **Offer incentives.** Can you provide bonuses or other enticements to facilitate on-time delivery?

- **Demand compliance.** Will insisting that people do what they said they would get the desired result? This may require support from upper management. Use this tactic selectively; be careful not to damage important relationships in pursuit of your goal.

noticed a decline in productivity at a satellite office. Or you might ask the product designers on your team to continue gathering among themselves on a biweekly basis because they've doubled their creative output since they've begun doing so. Keep the momentum going by following up each week on any to-dos and connecting them with the metrics for overall performance. Also, celebrate small successes along the way—that will rekindle the team's enthusiasm as you make progress toward your larger objectives.

Manage problems

Some problems have such far-reaching consequences that they can threaten the success of the entire project. Here are four of the biggest you'll face:

1. **Time slippage.** The most common problem in project management is falling behind schedule. Delays may be unavoidable, but you can usually at least improve the situation. The first step is to recognize that you're behind. If you've been monitoring the project's progress carefully, you'll quickly notice when schedules are being re-adjusted to accommodate delays or unexpected bottlenecks.

2. **Scope creep.** Time slippage can result from internal pressure to alter the scope of the project. When stakeholders ask for changes, it's your job to communicate clearly to them how those changes will affect cost, time, or quality.

   On some projects, scope creep is an ongoing battle for the project manager. After specific milestones and budgets have been agreed upon, people may begin to see more that could be achieved. Don't get caught up in trying to solve problems that lie beyond the established scope of your project—even ones that your company urgently needs to address.

3. **Quality issues.** Quality assurance plays a major role in any project's success. Unfortunately, it sometimes gives way to deadline pressure. Don't rush essential quality checks for the sake of the

schedule. And when you examine deliverables, use the most appropriate tools—such as detailed inspections, checklists, or statistical sampling—to accept or reject them. Return or rework rejected deliverables, depending on costs.

4. **People problems.** These are often the most difficult challenges a project manager must confront. They can generally be avoided or handled early on if you communicate frequently with each team member. Weekly staff meetings may not be enough; daily interaction—with individual team members or with the team as a whole—may be necessary.

Pay attention to small signs of emerging problems, such as a team member's increased tension and irritability, loss of enthusiasm, or inability to make decisions. When you see signs like these, get to the heart of the problem quickly and deal with it. Don't let it grow from a small irritant into a disaster.

Closeout: How to Handle End Matters

Though some projects *feel* endless, they all, eventually, come to a close. How do you, as project manager, know when to make that happen? And how do you go about it?

Evaluate project performance

Before closing out your project, your team needs to meet its goals (or determine, along with key stakeholders, that those goals no longer apply). Compare your progress with the scope everyone agreed on at the beginning. That

POST-EVALUATION REPORT

Sample Analysis and Lessons Learned

Project name: Project Phoenix   **Date:** 5/29/200X

Present at this session: Rafael, Phil, and Carmen

PROJECT PHASE/TASK

Equipment acquisition

What Worked

Obtained the Web servers on time and on budget.

What Didn't Work

Logistical problems with availability of database servers—caused a delay. Expedited order that introduced additional expense.

Ways to Improve

Need to order equipment earlier.

PROJECT PHASE/TASK

Provision and implement equipment

What Worked

Two days were recovered through the efforts of Rafael and Carmen during provisioning phase.

PROJECT PHASE/TASK

Test equipment

What Worked

Testing phase was successful; during testing, a bug in the database content was discovered and corrected prior to cutover.

PROJECT PHASE/TASK

Go live with new equipment

What Worked

Smooth cutover with minimal downtime.

What Didn't Work

Some users were unaware that there would be a brief outage.

Ways to Improve

Publicize work window to user base more aggressively.

PROJECT PHASE/TASK

Test again

What Worked

Tested fine.

PROJECT PHASE/TASK

Decommission old equipment

What Worked

Decommissioned sites and erased content successfully; reabsorbed stock into inventory.

What Didn't Work

Some confusion over serial numbers and inventory, but straightened out in the end.

Ways to Improve

Check serial numbers at an earlier phase to minimize problems at the end of project.

TARGET ANALYSIS

How well did the project/team do...

In achieving goals and meeting project objectives?

Success: all goals were achieved.

At meeting deadlines and the final completion date?

Success: met our target date.

At monitoring and staying within budget?

Success: slight overrun was unavoidable.

(continued)

TARGET ANALYSIS (CONTINUED)

How well did the project/team do...

At communicating with stakeholders?

Partial success: we could have done better at communicating requirements earlier to individuals involved in the phases of the project.

RESOURCES ASSESSMENT

Were the allocated resources appropriate, sufficient, and efficiently used? (i.e., time, people, money)

Generally, the resource allocations were appropriate. The project went slightly over budget, but was not inappropriate. The people involved had the expertise necessary to carry out the highly technical phases of the project. The time resources were appropriate as the project was completed on time with no room to spare.

LESSONS LEARNED

What are the key lessons learned that can be applied to future projects?

At each phase of the project, it is crucial to anticipate the next steps and to alert groups or individuals of resource requirements as early as possible in the process. By so doing, we probably could have acquired the equipment in a more timely manner and would not have had to scramble so much in the later phases to meet our target dates.

---

will tell you how well the project has performed—and if there's still work to do. When you discuss your findings with your stakeholders, make sure you reach consensus with them on how "finished" the project is. Keep your scope front and center so everyone uses the same yardstick to measure success.

Close the project

The steps you take to wrap things up will depend on whether your team assumes ownership of its own deliverables, hands them off to others in the organization, or must terminate the project altogether. Later in this guide, you'll learn about these three types of closeouts and some techniques you can use to make them go smoothly. If all has gone as planned with your project, then it's time for celebration. Even if, as is more likely, there are some rough spots along the way—the project takes longer than expected, the result is less than hoped for, or the costs overtake your estimates—it's still important to recognize the team's efforts and accomplishments.

Debrief with the team

No matter what the outcome, make sure you have scheduled a **post-evaluation**—time to debrief and document the process so that the full benefits of lessons learned can be shared. The post-evaluation is an opportunity for discovery, not for criticism and blame. Team members who fear they'll be punished for past problems may try to hide them rather than help find better ways of handling them in the future.

Develop a post-evaluation report

The post-evaluation report documents all information that will be useful not only for the current team and stakeholders but also for future project managers who may use it to plan their own projects. (See the sample report in this chapter.) It should include:

- **Insights from the team.** Which lessons identified during the debrief should be applied going forward?

A NOTE ABOUT PROJECT MANAGEMENT OFFICES

Large companies often have what's called a **Project Management Office** (PMO), which does some combination of the following:

- Establishes processes and templates to guide project managers in planning and execution.

- Provides coaching and assistance to business leaders, project managers, and team members trying to apply the processes and templates.

- Directly manages projects to achieve desired objectives. (PMOs in heavily matrixed organizations don't usually take on this responsibility.)

A PMO that's well run helps each project team develop an appropriate plan, conduct a reasonable risk estimate, and track progress—and it allows teams room to deviate from standard procedure when it makes sense to do so.

- **Future status.** What will happen to the project now that it has been completed? Was it part of a larger project, or was it a self-contained entity that completed its goals?

- **Status of ongoing critical tasks.** What is the current state of ongoing tasks that contain a high level of technical risk or are being performed by outside vendors or subcontractors?

- **Risk assessment.** Could or did any risks cause financial loss, project failure, or other liabilities?

- **Limitations of the audit.** Do you have any reason to question the validity of the post-evaluation? Is any information missing or suspect? Did anyone in the group seem to resist providing details?

Even after you've completed your project, you can draw on the knowledge you've gained, the skills you've learned, and the relationships you've formed. You've accumulated valuable assets. The trick is to keep using them as you begin new projects.

Chapter 2
The Cast of Characters

To meet your project objectives, you need the right people on board—and they must have a clear understanding of their roles. Here's a breakdown of who does what.

Sponsor

The **sponsor** champions the project at the highest level in the company and gets rid of organizational obstructions. She should have the clout to communicate effectively with the CEO and key stakeholders, provide necessary resources, and approve or reject outcomes. It's also important that she have "skin in the game"—in other words, accountability for the project's performance.

Project Manager

The **project manager** identifies the central problem to solve and determines, with input from the sponsor and

Adapted from *Harvard Business Essentials: Managing Projects Large and Small* (product #6198BC), Harvard Business Review Press, 2004

stakeholders, how to tackle it: what the project's objectives and scope will be and which activities will deliver the desired results. He then plans and schedules tasks, oversees day-to-day execution, and monitors progress until he evaluates performance, brings the project to a close, and captures the lessons learned. The project manager receives authority from the sponsor. In many respects, he's like a traditional manager because he must:

- Provide a framework for the project's activities

- Identify needed resources

- Negotiate with higher authorities

- Recruit effective participants

- Set milestones

- Coordinate activities

- Keep the vision clear and the work on track

- Make sure everyone on the team contributes and benefits

- Mediate conflicts

- Make sure project goals are delivered on time and on budget

Team Leader

Large projects may include a **team leader,** who reports directly to the project manager. In small projects, the project manager wears both hats. The team leader cannot act like the boss and still obtain the benefits of team-based work. Instead, he must adopt the following important roles:

- **Initiator.** Rather than tell people what to do, the leader draws attention to actions that must be taken for team goals to be met.

- **Model.** He uses his own behavior to shape others' performance—by starting meetings on time, for example, and following through on between-meeting assignments. Leaders often rely heavily on this tactic, since they typically cannot use promotions, compensation, or threats of dismissal to influence team members.

- **Negotiator.** He gets what he needs from resource providers by framing the project as mutually beneficial.

- **Listener.** He gathers from the environment signals of impending trouble, employee discontent, and opportunities for gain.

- **Coach.** He finds ways to help team members maximize their potential and achieve agreed-upon goals. Coaching opportunities are abundant within teams because the skills members eventually need are often ones they don't already have.

- **Working member.** In addition to providing direction, the leader must do a share of the work, particularly in areas where he has special competence. Ideally, he should also take on one or two of the unpleasant or unexciting jobs that no one else wants to do.

Team Members

The heart of any project, and the true engine of its work, is its membership. That's why bringing together the right people is extremely important.

Criteria for membership

Although the skills needed to accomplish the work should govern team selection, keep in mind that you're unlikely to get all the know-how you need without providing some training. Consider the following areas of proficiency:

- **Technical skills** in a specific discipline, such as market research, finance, or software programming

- **Problem-solving skills** enabling individuals to analyze difficult situations or impasses and to craft solutions

- **Interpersonal skills,** particularly the ability to collaborate effectively with others—a critical aspect of team-based work

- **Organizational skills,** including networking, communicating well with other parts of the company, and navigating the political landscape, all of which help the team get things done and avoid conflicts with operating units and their personnel

When forming project teams, people tend to focus too narrowly on technical skills and overlook interpersonal and organizational skills, which are just as important. For instance, a brilliant programmer may thwart team progress if she is unwilling to collaborate. By contrast, an organizationally savvy person with average technical skills may be the team's most valuable member, thanks to his ability to gather resources and enlist help from operating units.

Individuals who are strong on all four skill measures are few and far between. Make the most of the talent available, and take steps to neutralize weaknesses in your group. Look for people not just with valued skills but with the potential to learn new ones. Once you identify a candidate for membership, discuss her potential contribution with the sponsor. Consult her supervisor as well, since team membership absorbs time that would otherwise go toward regular assignments.

You may have to add new members and possibly bid thanks and good-bye to others over time, as tasks and needs change. One note of caution: Team members gradually develop effective patterns for working together, making decisions, and communicating. Cohesion is undermined when too many people join or exit the team.

Contributions and benefits

Free riders—team members who obtain the benefits of membership without doing their share—cannot be tolerated. However, not every member has to put in the same amount of time. For example, a senior manager who must direct much of his attention to other duties may still add value to the project by securing resources or by building support within the organization.

Just as each member must contribute to the team's work, each should receive clear benefits: a learning experience that will pay career dividends, for instance, or a fatter paycheck or bonus. Otherwise, individuals will not participate at a high level—at least not for long. The benefits they derive from their regular jobs will absorb their attention and make your project a secondary priority.

THE PROJECT STEERING COMMITTEE

Some projects have a **steering committee,** which consists of the sponsor and all key stakeholders. The committee's role is to approve the charter, secure resources, and adjudicate all requests to change key project elements, such as deliverables, the schedule, and the budget.

A steering committee is a good idea when different partnering companies, units, or individuals have a strong stake in the project. Because it represents these various interests, it is well positioned to sort out complicated interfirm or interdepartmental project problems. Likewise, it can be helpful if you anticipate many change requests. The downside to having a steering committee? It involves another level of oversight, and its meetings take up the time of some of the company's most expensive employees. So don't have a committee if you don't need one.

Alignment

The goals of the project team and those of its individual members must align with organizational objectives. For that reason, everyone's efforts should be coordinated through the company's rewards system. This kind of reinforcement begins at the top, with the sponsor. Since she is accountable for the team's success, some part of her compensation should be linked to the team's performance. Moving down the line, the project manager and team members should likewise see their compensation affected by team outcomes. Such alignment gets everyone moving in the same direction.

Phase 1
Planning

Chapter 3
A Written Charter

Every project should have a **charter** that spells out the nature and scope of the work and management's expectations for results. A charter is a concise written document containing some or all of the following:

- Name of the project's sponsor

- Project's benefits to the organization

- Brief description of the objectives

- Expected time frame

- Budget and resources available

- Project manager's authority

- Sponsor's signature

Creating a charter forces senior managers to clearly articulate what the project should do. Consider this example:

Adapted from *Harvard Business Essentials: Managing Projects Large and Small* (product #6211BC), Harvard Business Review Press, 2004

Phil was the sponsor of his company's effort to reengineer its order fulfillment and customer service operations. As an outspoken critic of these functions, he was the right person for the job. He had long been dissatisfied with the time it took to fill orders and with the company's mediocre customer service, and he thought the costs of these operations were too high. So he put Lila in charge of a project to improve them.

What sorts of cost cutting was Phil anticipating? What exactly were his complaints about the current system? What would success look like? Lila attempted to pin down Phil on those questions, but without success. He was too busy to think it all through and too eager to delegate responsibility for the project's outcome. Other company executives were also anxious to see improvements but, like Phil, had no clear ideas about the outcomes they wanted. So when Lila quizzed senior managers about the subject, they cited no specific goals. Lacking guidance, Lila and her team members developed their own goals and criteria for success.

The team pushed forward, and Lila reported progress to Phil over the course of the 10-month effort. Resources were always a problem, particularly since Lila was never sure how much money she could spend and how many people she could add to the team at key stages. Every request for resources had to be negotiated on a case-by-case basis with Phil.

The team eventually completed its tasks, meeting all of its self-declared goals. It had cut order-fulfillment time by one-third and the overall costs of fulfillment and customer service by 12%. And 90%

*of customers could now get all their issues resolved
with a single phone call. The team celebrated with a
splendid dinner, and members went back to their regular duties.*

*Senior management, however, was not entirely
pleased with the outcome. "You did a pretty good job,"
Phil told Lila. "The improvements you've made are
significant, but we were looking for a more sweep-
ing reorganization and larger cost savings." Lila was
stunned and more than slightly angry. "If he wanted
these things," she thought, "why didn't he say so?"*

Situations like this are common but can be avoided
with a charter that clarifies the project's objectives, time
frame, and scope.

Objectives

As Lila's case demonstrates, project managers need
more than a broad-brush description of the objectives
for which they will be responsible. Ambiguous goals can
lead to misunderstandings, disappointment, and expensive rework.

Take, for instance, the following statement: "Develop
a website that's capable of providing fast, accurate product information and fulfillment to our customers in a
cost-effective way." What exactly does that mean? What
is "fast"? How should accuracy be defined? Is one error
in 1,000 transactions acceptable? One in 10,000? To
what degree must the site be cost-effective? Each of those
questions should be answered in consultation with the
project's sponsor and key stakeholders.

A thoughtful charter specifies the ends, but the means should be left to the project manager and team members. Telling the team what it should do *and* how to do it would undermine the benefits of having recruited a competent group. As J. Richard Hackman writes in *Leading Teams*: "When ends are specified but means are not, team members are able to—indeed, are implicitly encouraged to—draw on their full complement of knowledge, skill, and experience in devising and executing a way of operating that is well tuned to the team's purpose and circumstances."

Time Frame

In addition to setting specific, measurable objectives, you'll need to establish a time frame for achieving them. The project cannot be open-ended. In some cases, the deadline must be firm, and the scope becomes variable. Suppose a software company promises to deliver a new release every three months. The project team must make adjustments to the scope of its new releases—adding or dropping product features—to meet each deadline.

By contrast, if the project's scope is fixed, then a logical deadline can be established only after the project manager and team break down the objectives into sets of tasks and estimate the duration of each task. Nevertheless, the charter should contain a reasonable deadline—one that can be amended as the project team learns more about what it must do.

Scope

Of course, options are always more plentiful than time and resources. One useful technique for making the right choices is to have key stakeholders and project participants join in a brainstorming exercise to define what should be within scope and what should not.

Think of the sponsor's expectations (the ends to be sought) as part one of the charter and the project plan (the means) as part two. The project manager typically creates the plan, but it's important to get the sponsor's approval on it so you don't run into the same problems Lila faced with Phil. Ideally, it represents the best ideas from many or all team members. It's especially valuable for large, complex endeavors because it provides details about tasks, deliverables, risks, and timetables. It serves as a road map for the team.

Chapter 4
Dealing with a Project's "Fuzzy Front End"

by Loren Gary

Project management used to be about driving out uncertainty. You nailed down all the deliverables at the outset and fine-tuned your specs so implementation could be as routine as possible. Sure, there were always a few surprises, but overall you had a pretty good idea of what to expect. In many of today's complex projects, however—whether they involve new-product development, IT installation, or internal process improvement—uncertainty simply can't be eliminated.

If you were retooling a shoe company's manufacturing plant, says David Schmaltz, a Washington-based project management consultant, "perhaps only 10% of the

---

Adapted from *Harvard Management Update* (product #U0306C), June 2003 work would be devoted to building the new production line, but 50% would have to do with the uncertainty surrounding which shoe style will sell best in the next quarter. . . . Thus, instead of trying to cut its time to market by building production lines faster, the company focuses on building production lines that can more easily accommodate changing shoe styles."

Studies of exceptional project managers in fast time-to-market industries show that the initial phase of a complex project, often referred to as the **fuzzy front end,** has a disproportionately large impact on end results. So it's important to tread carefully. Resist the urge to dive right into implementation. "Defining the problem first gives you greater degrees of freedom in solving it," says Bob Gill, president of the Product Development and Management Association, a New Jersey–based nonprofit. "Instead of assuming that your riveting equipment is operating too slowly, if you step back and say, 'The real issue is that my cost of manufacturing the product is too high,' you enable other possible alternatives to solving the problem—for example, redesigning the process so that the product requires fewer rivets."

Build Your Community Early

You'll need input from key stakeholders before you can reach a robust understanding of the nature and scope of what needs to be done. Ask people in various groups likely to be affected by your project to help explore the opportunities, advises Peter Koen, a professor at the Stevens Institute of Technology, also in New Jersey. "Asking up front the questions about the unmet needs and the value of what you're doing can help prevent unsatisfactory results down the road—for example, bringing out products to a mature and declining market."

As you invite others into the work of defining the problem, you'll soon realize that your project's community is much larger than you originally imagined. And it will shift over time, points out Chuck Kolstad, CEO of Antara, a high-tech firm in California. "Stakeholders who have only informational input into the early phases of the project may wield decision-making power later on." If you make it clear in those early days that you value their insights and will incorporate them, your stakeholders will be much more inclined to give you the buy-in you need. Here's where your recruitment skills come into play: As you share your developing vision for the project with a colleague whose assistance you'll need, ask her what's in it for her. Help her find her project within yours.

Assuming a typical complex project, which lasts less than a year, "the week or two you spend at the outset just having conversations with people is far from useless, despite its appearance," says Schmaltz. When plans slip or new requirements are added, he continues, the relationships you've built during this initial phase will "constitute a benevolent conspiracy of people committed to figuring out how to make the project work."

Work Backward

Research about cognitive bias has shown that decision makers are unduly influenced by how they initially frame their thoughts about a topic. Once you've defined the problem, don't focus yet on the current process or product you want to improve. Instead, says Jim Goughenhour, vice president of information technology at Sealy, "imagine what the ideal end state would look like, then work back to put in as much of it as you can given the time, budget, and political realities."

The traditional approach to one of the projects Goughenhour oversees—creating a consistent sales reporting system—would have been to revisit the purpose of all the existing reports used by sales and marketing people throughout the company and explore ways of combining them. "If we'd done that," he says, "we'd have spent most of our money making minor improvements that didn't come close to the ideal."

Be the Voice of Reason

By the end of the project's initial phase, you'll produce a general plan that sets expectations within the project community and the company at large. That's certainly no small task, but it can be an even bigger challenge to manage the expectations of your sponsor—the project champion three or four levels above you who insists that the work be completed in four weeks.

Remember your "sacred responsibility to disappoint," says Schmaltz. You know that unsettling hunch you've got, now that the fuzzy-front-end conversations are winding down, that the project will take much longer than expected and will cost a lot more, too? "Only by disappointing the project champion with this news in the beginning can you delight him in the end," Schmaltz says.

"Otherwise you end up being a slave to his unrealistic expectations, and instead of guaranteeing success, you're almost certain to produce failure."

Loren Gary was the editor of *Harvard Management Update.*

Chapter 5
Performing a Project *Pre*mortem

by Gary Klein

Projects fail at a spectacular rate. One reason is that too many people are reluctant to speak up about their reservations during the all-important planning phase. By making it safe for dissenters who are knowledgeable about the undertaking and worried about its weaknesses to speak up, you can improve a project's chances of success.

Research conducted in 1989 by Deborah J. Mitchell, of the Wharton School; Jay Russo, of Cornell; and Nancy Pennington, of the University of Colorado, found that prospective hindsight—imagining that an event has already occurred—increases the ability to correctly identify reasons for future outcomes by 30%. We have used prospective hindsight to devise a method called a *premortem*, which helps project teams identify risks at the outset.

Reprint #F0709A. To order, visit hbr.org.

A premortem is the hypothetical opposite of a post-mortem. A postmortem in a medical setting allows health professionals and the family to learn what caused a patient's death. Everyone benefits except, of course, the patient. A premortem in a business setting comes at the beginning of a project rather than the end, so that the project can be improved rather than autopsied. Unlike a typical critiquing session, in which project team members are asked what *might* go wrong, the premortem operates on the assumption that the "patient" has died, and so asks what *did* go wrong. The team members' task is to generate plausible reasons for the project's failure.

A typical premortem begins after the team has been briefed on the plan. The leader starts the exercise by informing everyone that the project has failed spectacularly. Over the next few minutes those in the room independently write down every reason they can think of for the failure—especially the kinds of things they ordinarily wouldn't mention as potential problems, for fear of being impolitic. For example, in a session held at one *Fortune* 50–size company, an executive suggested that a billion-dollar environmental sustainability project had "failed" because interest waned when the CEO retired. Another pinned the failure on a dilution of the business case after a government agency revised its policies.

Next the leader asks each team member, starting with the project manager, to read one reason from his or her list; everyone states a different reason until all have been recorded. After the session is over, the project manager reviews the list, looking for ways to strengthen the plan.

In a session regarding a project to make state-of-the-art computer algorithms available to military air-campaign planners, a team member who had been silent during the previous lengthy kickoff meeting volunteered that one of the algorithms wouldn't easily fit on certain laptop computers being used in the field. Accordingly, the software would take hours to run when users needed quick results. Unless the team could find a workaround, he argued, the project was impractical. It turned out that the algorithm developers had already created a powerful shortcut, which they had been reluctant to mention. Their shortcut was substituted, and the project went on to be highly successful.

In a session assessing a research project in a different organization, a senior executive suggested that the project's "failure" occurred because there had been insufficient time to prepare a business case prior to an upcoming corporate review of product initiatives. During the entire 90-minute kickoff meeting, no one had even mentioned any time constraints. The project manager quickly revised the plan to take the corporate decision cycle into account.

Although many project teams engage in prelaunch risk analysis, the premortem's prospective hindsight approach offers benefits that other methods don't. Indeed, the premortem doesn't just help teams to identify potential problems early on. It also reduces the kind of damn-the-torpedoes attitude often assumed by people who are overinvested in a project. Moreover, in describing weaknesses that no one else has mentioned, team members feel valued for their intelligence and experience, and others learn from them. The exercise also sensitizes the team to pick up early signs of trouble once the project gets under way. In the end, a premortem may be the best way to circumvent any need for a painful postmortem.

Gary Klein is a senior scientist at MacroCognition, in Yellow Springs, Ohio.

Chapter 6
Will Project Creep Cost You— or Create Value?

by Loren Gary

Allow the wrong changes to your project, and you can veer off course, run over budget, and miss key deadlines. Reject the right change, and you may fail to capitalize on a major opportunity. Hence the dilemma: How do you stay open to improvements without succumbing to "creep," in which small tweaks add up to budget- or schedule-busting modifications? By making sure the project's boundaries are sharply delineated and the impact of potential alterations or slippage can be quickly calculated.

The Planning Phase

A surprising number of projects get under way without a thorough attempt to define parameters. Haste is the chief

Adapted from *Harvard Management Update* (product #U0501C), January 2005 culprit here, says Dave Moffatt, who brings 40 years of industry project-management experience to his role as senior operations adviser at Harvard Business School (HBS). As you plan your project, clarify it in the following important ways:

Differentiate scope from purpose

"A project's purpose is the general benefit it will provide to the organization," explains Alex Walton, a Florida-based project consultant. "Its scope comprises the particular elements (or product attributes) that the project team can control and has agreed to deliver."

For example, a project's purpose may be to create a new electronic game that will increase a toy company's holiday sales by 40%. But the team developing the product needs to know what features it must have and what the budget for producing it will be. The **scope statement** provides this kind of information; it spells out, in a few sentences, how the team intends to achieve success and, thus, the criteria on which it will be evaluated. Get input on scope from your key stakeholders to align their expectations with the project's actual trajectory.

Plan in the aggregate

Defining scope isn't enough to ensure clear boundaries, however. "Organizations also need to do aggregate project planning," says HBS professor Steven Wheelwright, "in which they develop a strategy that lays out a pattern and rhythm for when subsequent projects will occur." This is especially important for product development.

Lacking a schedule for future projects, a product engineer with a new idea may grow concerned that it will never be implemented and thus try to slip it into the product that's now in development—regardless of the impact on the cost and schedule.

Analysis of prior projects serves as a valuable adjunct to aggregate planning. Study the past several internal IT projects your company has undertaken. What patterns emerge? Your findings can help you identify and better prepare for potential trouble spots in IT projects on the docket for the coming years.

Set the rules

Another way to minimize creep is to require conscious discussion and approval before significant changes can occur. For instance:

- **Set up a change control board.** In highly structured project environments, such a group is responsible for "gathering information about the impact that a proposed change will have on the schedule, budget, or scope; voting on the proposed change; and then sending a request-for-change document on for the project sponsors' signature," says Bob Tarne, a senior consultant who specializes in IT and telecommunications projects for PM Solutions in Pennsylvania.

  For an IT project affecting the sales, marketing, and logistics departments, your change control board would contain senior managers from those units. Smaller projects—costing less than $1 million and lasting less than 12 months—can effectively function without a formal board, says Tarne. The project manager can simply solicit the advice of key stakeholders as needed.

- **Establish thresholds for additional work.**
  Michele Reed, an independent project management consultant in Washington, says, "Any change entailing more than 5% of the original cost or hours budgeted for that particular line item in the project should trigger a formal request for a scope change."

- **Limit the number of new features.** Set guidelines for how many new major and minor features can be included in a project of a certain size. This helps the project team control the inherent fuzziness of front-end planning by forcing it to choose only the ones that are most important to customers right now.

The Execution Phase

When it's time to implement the project, break it into small components with short time frames and focus first on the tasks with the least uncertainty and variability.

For example, a software development team working on a product with four new features—the fourth of which it is not yet sure the market really wants—might choose to create the other three first because it is confident that the market wants them. The launch date for the fourth feature would be set to occur later, after the team has gathered enough additional customer input to confirm that it is critical.

But don't wait until all subprojects are complete before checking on whether the whole project (or product) is going to be a success, says Wheelwright. He recommends an approach known as **periodic system prototyping:** "At regular intervals during the execution phase, link up all the subprojects for a system test. This helps ensure that the subprojects you've created are coming together as planned."

Should *This* Add-On Be Approved?

During construction of McArthur Hall, HBS's residence for students in executive education programs (some of which last as long as eight weeks), a scope-change decision was made to create 10 rooms so guests of attendees could visit for a few days at a time.

Reducing the number of rooms for students by 10 would have cut into the program's long-term revenue potential by reducing the available space for registrants. Better to build 10 additional rooms to accommodate guests, the project's executive sponsor argued, and to pay for the additional cost over several years out of the larger income stream that would result from keeping the number of exec-ed suites as originally planned. Careful ROI analysis, in other words, helped the project's overseers find the optimal way of dealing with the proposed add-on.

By following the recommendations outlined here for your project's planning and execution phases, you can eliminate scope changes that don't merit such analysis. If you define clear boundaries up front, the change requests that come through are much more likely to be worth serious consideration.

When considering a scope change, make sure your stakeholders fully understand the purpose of the change. For example, have market conditions made it important to accelerate the schedule so that the product can ship earlier than originally planned? Do new industry standards, adopted since the planning phase, need to be accommodated? Or is a new technological solution required, because the one initially chosen hasn't panned out?

Next, explain how the proposed change affects everything: the scope statement and project plan, the available resources, the total cost, and the schedule. Finally, encourage stakeholders to consider what will happen if the change is not made. In these deliberations, says HBS's Moffatt, the opinions of people who represent the end users should be given the greatest weight.

As the project manager, if you're lobbying for a change, you've got to have a plan for funding it. If the future revenue generated by the add-on won't cover the cost, find other places in the project where you can save money, and focus on things you can directly control within the next 30 to 90 days in the schedule, advises Reed.

Loren Gary was the editor of *Harvard Management Update.*

Phase 2
Build-Up

Chapter 7
Setting Priorities Before Starting Your Project

by Ron Ashkenas

In a rush to demonstrate initiative and take action, new project managers often launch activities without first getting a sense of which ones are the most critical and what the sequence should be. As a result, they unwittingly slow things down.

Take this example: Plant managers at a global manufacturing company kept getting peppered with unnecessary, often redundant, data requests from corporate headquarters. To reduce this burden, the head of manufacturing asked a senior engineer to lead a project team to streamline data sharing. Upon receiving the assignment, the engineer enthusiastically (1) fired off an e-mail requesting that all heads of corporate functions nominate team members and send lists of the data they wanted from the plants; and (2) sent a note to a dozen plant managers asking for their views about which re-ports to eliminate. Within hours, the new project man-ager was overwhelmed and confused: Some of the cor-porate executives balked at her requests because this was the first they'd even heard of the project; others said they needed more details about the problem before they could respond; and still others sent long lists of required re-ports. The plant managers, too, came back with an odd mix of questions and requests. So instead of getting off to a fast start, the project manager stirred up resistance, created extra work for herself and others, and ended up with a pile of information that wasn't very useful.

It's not as difficult as you might think to avoid a situ-ation like this. Here are three simple steps you can take to get your priorities right before you set your project in motion:

1. Clarify the assignment

Do not start any activities until your stakeholders have blessed your charter. You can easily spin your wheels on all sorts of misguided tasks if you're not clear on the overall objectives of the project and how success will be measured (what); the business context for it (why); the resources available (who); the timing (when); and any key constraints or interdependencies (how). Though it would be nice if your boss or project sponsor had sorted out these issues *before* giving you the assignment, the reality is that most projects are not commissioned with this level of specificity and clarity—so it will be up to you to get it. In the example above, if the project manager had done this before sending e-mails, she would have discovered that the head of manufacturing had talked only in general terms to the other corporate functional leaders about the data-overload problem—and had not told them he was starting a specific project with a defined goal and timetable.

2. Organize your troops

Once you've figured out what needs to be accomplished and recruited team members, get people engaged quickly so they feel ownership of the project. Ask for their reactions to the charter and their experiences regarding the issues, and treat them as partners rather than temporary subordinates. Work with them to develop a "modus operandi" for your team—how often you will meet, how you will communicate with one another, when you will review progress with the sponsor, and so on. If you don't get organized from the beginning, you'll waste time later chasing down people, coordinating calendars, and repeating key messages.

The same goes for identifying and reaching out to stakeholders. Have your team help you create a "map" of the people who will be affected in some way by the project. Sketch out how they relate to one another and to the project—and then do a political analysis of the key players. Which individuals or groups will be supportive and enthusiastic about your project? Which ones might be anxious or even resistant? Who will need to be won over or given special attention? Such analysis would have revealed to the project manager in our manufacturing example that some (or all) of the corporate functional leaders—who would have to

> ## SAMPLE CHARTER FOR
> ## DATA-STREAMLINING PROJECT
>
> **What:** Reduce corporate's requests for data from plants by 50%—and free up at least four hours per week for the plant managers and staff.
>
> **Why:** The plants need to focus on increasing equipment utilization while managing a greater mix of products. This means spending more time planning and leading and less time reporting. Currently, every corporate function is asking for information from the plants—often the same information in different forms at different times.
>
> **Who:** The project manager will recruit team members from plant operations, corporate finance, quality assurance, and human resources. Others may be called upon as necessary. All members will

change their way of collecting data to comply with her requests—would not be supportive of her project and may in fact be hostile. And with that insight, she might have approached them differently.

3. Pull your project plan together

You're now ready to develop a project plan, or at least a good working draft, given what you know about your objectives and your stakeholders. Conduct a brainstorming session with your team to identify all the activities that be part-time but may have to dedicate 25% of their time to this effort.

When: The project should commence immediately. Develop an inventory of current reporting requirements within 30 days and recommendations for consolidation and streamlining within 60 days. Start eliminating redundant reports within 90 days. Complete implementation within 120 days.

How: The corporate functions must reach consensus about which common data requests can be met with existing systems and standardized reports. Data requests that are unique for particular plants should be exceptions, not the rule, and should involve minimal customization.

might be required to complete the project—including data collection, completion of "quick wins," stakeholder meetings, and presentations. Encourage your team to be creative and not to worry at this point about timing. Write each item on a sticky note, and post the notes on the wall.

Once all the activities are up there, organize them into categories and put the groupings in sequence. Some of the categories will "run" in parallel and represent separate (but probably related) work streams.

The notes on the wall, taken together, represent your project plan.

Now take a hard look at that total picture. Give each team member 100 "units" to allocate to the various activities (without discussion); ask them to pay close attention to which ones *must* be done successfully to achieve the project's objectives. Then compare the allocations and see which activities are considered critical as opposed to "nice to do." This should lead you to the tough discussion of which ones to drop or delay so the highest priorities will get the focus and the resources they require. After you've completed this exercise, go back to the overall project plan and make the necessary adjustments: Remove the low-value steps, and load the high-value ones for success.

Clearly, it's counterproductive to get things moving without prioritizing tasks. But controlling the all-too-natural impulse to jump the gun only at the beginning of your project is not sufficient. New opportunities, issues, ideas, and threats will continue to materialize, as will new steps and work streams—often without anyone understanding how these items even made their way onto the table. You'll need to keep setting and resetting priorities to make sure you and your people are always on target. To do this, bring your team together at least once a month to step back and reassess the project plan. At each of these meetings, ask your team two questions: First, "Has anything changed that should make us rethink our priorities?" And second, "If we were just given this assignment now, would we approach it differently?" This will help you keep your priorities clear—and your project on track.

———————

Ron Ashkenas is a senior partner at Schaffer Consulting in Stamford, Connecticut, and the author of *Simply Effective: How to Cut Through Complexity in Your Organization and Get Things Done* (Harvard Business Review Press, 2009). He is a regular blogger for hbr.org.

Chapter 8
Boost Productivity with Time-Boxing

by Melissa Raffoni

Editor's note: To keep your project on schedule, you'll need team members who are focused and productive. Here are some tips for getting their calendars—and your own—under control.

Everybody needs more time—but since no one gets more than 24 hours a day, the only choice is to use those hours more effectively. One proven technique, time-boxing, involves just three steps.

First, list everything you and your team members want to accomplish in a given week, month, or quarter. Include project goals and the tasks necessary to achieve them. It may help to group activities by job function, such as strategy, business development, daily operations,

---

Adapted from *Harvard Management Update* (product #U99120), December 1999

and people management. With that kind of framework, you can see whether the team is spending its time in the right places.

Second, estimate how much time each item will require. Think carefully about the steps for completing the tasks. This is the part that "keeps me honest," says Beran Peter, CEO of Instruction Set, an educational consulting company in Massachusetts. "If I realize I'm not going to hit my estimate, I'm able to assess why and evaluate how I might make a change to get back on track."

Third, block off the appropriate amount of time for each item. If you think writing a business plan will take 32 hours, try setting aside four hours for every Tuesday and Thursday over the next four weeks. The challenge, of course, is prioritizing and fitting the time in where it makes sense. Don't forget to allow some leeway. Change is inevitable, and you may need to add tasks midstream.

Once you get started on time-boxing, you'll find it has several benefits:

- It forces you to think through project goals and figure out how much time you really need to make them happen.

- It provides a framework for setting expectations and boundaries. If a team member's calendar is full, she'll have to say no to extra requests—or you'll have to work with her to consciously reassess priorities.

- It improves your ability to estimate time demands.

- It enables you to assess—and pull the plug on—unproductive initiatives that suck up too much time.

Your team will feel better about the work it's doing. Everyone will be more focused. You'll all accomplish more. And—no small matter—people will avoid burnout from taking on more than they can handle.

Chapter 9
Scheduling the Work

Now that you've used the Work Breakdown Structure to identify and define your project's tasks and estimate how long each will take, you're ready to put them in sequence. That involves three steps:

- Examining relationships between tasks

- Creating a draft schedule

- Optimizing the schedule

Examining Relationships Between Tasks

Task relationships dictate the order of activities in a project. Suppose ABC Auto Company plans to introduce a new passenger car and has asked a team to design and test it. The team needs to build and test both external

Adapted from *Harvard Business Essentials: Managing Projects Large and Small* (product #6242BC), Harvard Business Review Press, 2004, and *Pocket Mentor: Managing Projects* (product #1878), Harvard Business Review Press, 2006 and internal components before it can test the whole car. Because of those dependencies, the project's tasks must be scheduled in this sequence: (1) design the vehicle, (2) build and test both external and internal components, and (3) test the vehicle built from those components. (See figure 1.)

Component building and testing, however, can simultaneously follow parallel tracks—one for external components, another for internal ones. Why? Because those two sets of build-and-test activities depend on vehicle design but not on each other. By recognizing opportunities to perform different activities in parallel, as in this example, you can reduce the amount of time your overall project takes.

Once you've evaluated the relationships between tasks, brainstorm with your team to come up with a rough sequence that makes sense in light of the dependencies you've identified.

FIGURE 1

Project network diagram: task relationships

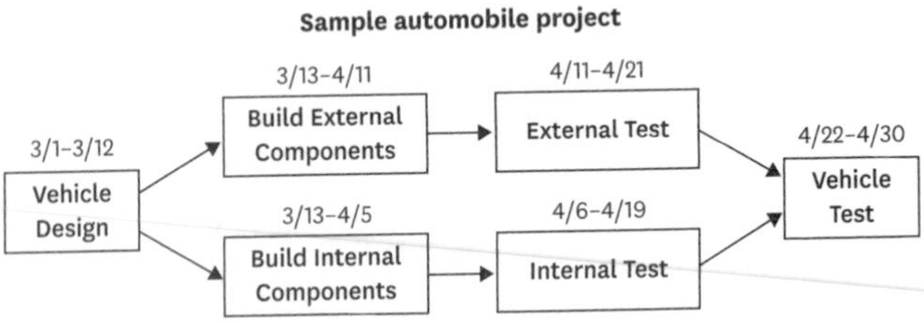

Sample automobile project

Source: Harvard ManageMentor® on Project Management (Boston: Harvard Business Publishing, 2002). Used with permission.

Creating a Draft Schedule

At this point, you're ready to create a draft schedule, which involves assigning a deliverable to each task (for instance, "build prototype for market testing"); setting realistic due dates; identifying bottlenecks so you can eliminate them, develop workarounds, or add time to accommodate them; and establishing a protocol for updating or revising the schedule. In your draft schedule, indicate start and end dates for all activities and recognize task relationships. Remember, this is just your first stab at scheduling—you'll make adjustments later, after the team has had a chance to review it.

Project managers rely on several tools for scheduling their teams' work. Here are a few useful ones to have at your disposal.

The Critical Path Method

As its name suggests, the **Critical Path Method (CPM)** helps you identify which tasks are critical—those that must be completed on time for the project to meet its deadlines—so you can allocate resources efficiently. Project managers often use CPM to plot the sequence of activities.

Consider a project involving six tasks with the following requirements and time expectations:

Activity	Requirement	Time to Complete
A		5 days
B		3 days

(continued)

Activity	Requirement	Time to Complete
C	A and B completed	4 days
D	B completed	7 days
E	A completed	6 days
F	C completed	4 days

You can diagram the critical path as shown in figure 2.

This chart tells you that at the earliest, you can complete the project in 11 days. It also shows that activities A and E are critical to your overall deadline. Given this information, you may want to readjust your resources and put more toward these tasks.

Let's revisit the ABC Auto Company project and the accompanying **network diagram,** discussed earlier. The diagram not only illustrates dependencies between tasks but also reveals the critical path: (1) vehicle design, (2) build external components, (3) external test, and (4) vehicle test. Why does this progression of tasks define the critical path? Because it's the longest path in the diagram. The other path—which passes through (1) build

FIGURE 2

Critical Path Method

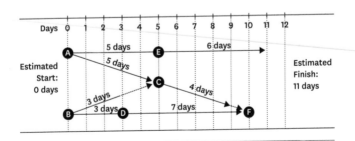

internal components and (2) internal test—is shorter by two days. Team members working on those activities could spend two extra days on them and still not throw the vehicle test off schedule. And they wouldn't shorten the overall schedule if they completed their work on non-critical-path activities ahead of time. The reason? **Tasks on the critical path determine total project duration.**

Gantt chart

If all you need is a way to show when activities should begin and when they should end, try making a **Gantt chart.** You can easily create one with spreadsheet or project-management software. (See figure 3.)

This is a popular scheduling tool because it's simple and it allows people to see the project at a glance. But it does not spell out relationships between tasks, as CPM does, so you may want to make note of dependencies inside the time blocks.

PERT charts

Some project managers use **Performance Evaluation and Review Technique** (**PERT**) as an alternative to the Gantt method for scheduling. Because it illustrates the critical path (it's essentially a network diagram) and lays out the project milestones, it's a handy tool for communicating the big picture to your team members. (See figure 4.) A PERT chart may have many parallel or interconnecting networks of tasks, so periodic reviews are essential for complex projects. As you're tracking your project's progress later on, you may need to come back and revise the chart. For example, if the time between dependent tasks exceeds your estimates, and those

FIGURE 3

Gantt chart

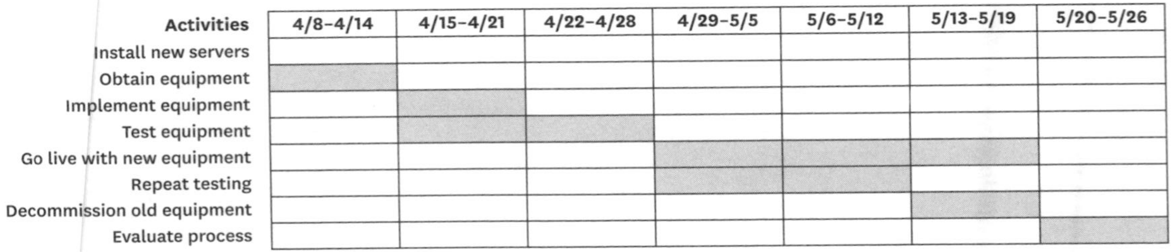

Activities	4/8–4/14	4/15–4/21	4/22–4/28	4/29–5/5	5/6–5/12	5/13–5/19	5/20–5/26
Install new servers	▓						
Obtain equipment		▓					
Implement equipment		▓					
Test equipment			▓				
Go live with new equipment				▓	▓	▓	
Repeat testing					▓		
Decommission old equipment						▓	
Evaluate process							▓

Source: Harvard ManageMentor® on Project Management (Boston: Harvard Business Publishing, 2002), 26. Used with permission.

FIGURE 4

PERT chart

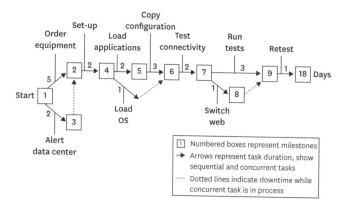

Source: Harvard ManageMentor® on Project Management (Boston: Harvard Business Publishing, 2002), 25. Used with permission.

tasks are on the critical path, you'll have to make up for lost time elsewhere in the schedule to avoid missing the project's overall deadline.

Which scheduling tools are best for your purposes? Whichever ones fit how you like to work, allow you to keep all team members informed, and remind people that they are part of a larger effort.

Optimizing the Schedule

After you've created the draft schedule, work with your team to improve it. Have the group help you look for:

- **Errors.** Are all time estimates realistic? Pay particular attention to tasks on the critical path because if any of these cannot be completed on time, the entire schedule will be off. Also, review the relationships between tasks. Does your schedule reflect the fact that some tasks can't start until others are completed?

- **Oversights.** Have any tasks been left out? Have you allowed time for training?

- **Overcommitments.** In reviewing the schedule, you may discover that some employees would have to work 10 to 12 hours per day for months on end to complete the tasks assigned to them, for instance, or that a piece of equipment is booked to deliver above and beyond its capacity. If you find such problems, redistribute the load.

- **Bottlenecks.** Any task that causes the work feeding it to pile up must be identified and dealt with. Think of an auto assembly line that stops periodically because the people who install the seats cannot keep up with the pace of the line. The usual way to handle this problem is to speed up the work process used in that task or add resources to it (for example, more people or better machinery).

- **Imbalances in the workload.** Are some team members being asked to do more than their share while others do very little? Rebalancing the load could reduce the overall schedule.

- **Slack time that can be filled.** You may be able to shorten the whole schedule by shifting resources away from noncritical-path activities. For example, if you have four people working on a noncritical task that has four to five days of slack time, shift some or all of those people to a critical task for several days.

Even if you're using project-planning software to keep track of tasks and times, do this kind of thorough reality check with your team members. Any software you consider buying should make it easy to develop and change charts, calculate critical paths, produce schedules and budgets, factor in weekends and holidays, create different scenarios for contingency planning, and check for overscheduling of individuals and groups.

Chapter 10
HBR Case Study: A Rush to Failure?

by Tom Cross

> *Editor's note:* HBR's case studies present fictionalized accounts of actual dilemmas faced by leaders, and offer solutions from experts.

"There is absolutely no reason why the contractors shouldn't be able to give us rapid product development and flawless products—speed and quality both," David MacDonagle said as he tried to light a cigarette. The warm wind, portending rain, kept blowing out his matches. Finally he gave up and slipped the cigarette back in his pocket.

MacDonagle, the head of the Canadian Aeronautics Administration, was nervous. Everyone at CAA headquarters was nervous. Very shortly, the project that many of them had devoted the past four years to would have its first real-world test, 350 kilometers above the earth.

Reprint #R1104N. Reprint Case only #R1104X. Reprint Commentary only #R1104Z

Feeling cooped up in the executive offices and oppressed by the presence of the media, MacDonagle had gone outside to breathe some air—actually, some tobacco smoke—and had invited the sharp young program manager Samantha Van Sant to join him.

Van Sant, a former Canadian army major, had a lot of skin in the project too. Since 2006 she'd been managing the two contractors the CAA had commissioned to build the $1.2 billion set of giant robotic arms known as Retractable Extended-Arms Compatible Holder, or REACH, for the International Space Station.

"So how do you deal with nerves?" MacDonagle asked.

"I usually go out for a run," Van Sant said, looking down the road that led from CAA headquarters through the cornfields, on which she'd logged many miles.

They turned to look back at the agency's buildings, which despite their grandeur looked small in the empty Quebec landscape. The sight reminded Van Sant of one of MacDonagle's catchphrases: "We are a small spacefaring nation. . . ."

Canada was indeed a small player in space compared with the U.S., Russia, Europe, and Japan. Always at risk of being marginalized, the CAA had done everything possible to get the REACH contractors, Hollenbeck Aircraft and Eskina Software Systems, to complete the first phase of the project in time to get it to the space station this year, when the orbiting lab would officially be complete. And, amazingly, they had made the deadline—and come in on budget. REACH was now attached to the station, though there was still much more to come, including an even more sophisticated set of "hands" that would fit on the ends of the robotic arms for extremely delicate work. The additions were to continue for two more years.

The contractors had been great about speed; the problem was quality. Glitches with the software, motors, and circuits had kept turning up. The fact was, not a single test in four years had gone flawlessly. "Yeah, yeah, we can fix that," the contractors' reps always said, dismissing the CAA's concerns. "Hey, this is life in the fast lane," a rep told Van Sant after one of REACH's arms had failed to retract on command. "Remember, we told you that the compressed schedule would increase the risk."

The contract that she managed called for parallel development, meaning that the project's phases—R&D, prototyping, testing, production, and quality control—overlapped, with each one beginning while the previous one was as much as 50% incomplete. That was sacrilege in some aerospace circles. But owing to the space station's construction deadline and the everpresent threat of cuts to the CAA's budget, the agency was aiming to do a decade's worth of work in six years. Computer simulations had to take the place of some real-world testing. Component quality control was less thorough. Because of all the unknowns in the project, the CAA had agreed to a cost-plus-fixed-fee contract, under which the contractors were paid a specified amount over their costs for labor, materials, and overhead.

MacDonagle's insistence on a rapid approach to development had been one of the main reasons Van Sant had been hired as a program manager. During her years in the army, she had established a bulletproof reputation for being aggressive and goal oriented. She and MacDonagle saw eye-to-eye. She knew speed was critical.

"We'd better go, I guess," MacDonagle said. "The media hounds are waiting. I told them I'd do quickie interviews once I got back. I know what they'll ask me: Is REACH going to work this time?" As they headed toward the building, the rain started. He looked at Van Sant. "So is it?"

Trouble in the Air

Red marker in hand, MacDonagle held forth before a group of reporters, asking whether they were aware that 50 years ago, the U.S. had blasted half a billion inch-long copper needles into orbit to reflect radio waves and thereby facilitate communications. Those needles were still floating around, and some had torn through one of the space station's solar collectors. "The solar arrays are the big bird's big red wings," he said, turning to the whiteboard and drawing the collectors.

He drew a gash in one of them. "A hole here means less electricity," he said, tapping the board. "Ever since the solar array got that hole from those flying needles, the space station has been operating on less power. Fixing it is tricky, because it's very far from the modules where the astronauts work and because of the risk of electrocution. Once an array is in place, you can't turn it off. It keeps generating power from sunlight. So if a spacewalker were to try to go out there and fix it, he'd be liable to get 100 volts of direct current through his body. That's where REACH comes in."

He took a moment to draw the Canadian creation, then stepped back to admire his sketch. The machine's two long arms stretched out toward the solar array in a nurturing embrace.

"Fixing solar arrays isn't what REACH was designed for," MacDonagle said. "It's meant to do the mundane work of replacing battery units on the exterior of the space station. But since REACH is up there, it's being pressed into service for the repair. It will stitch together the solar array while the astronauts control it from the safety of their module." He put the cap back on the marker and began fielding questions.

As Van Sant watched, someone tapped her on the arm. It was Alfred Siroy, the head of a CAA panel that had been trying to find out why there were so many quality issues with equipment from the Hollenbeck-Eskina venture.

"How long before they deploy it?" he asked.

"Soon—later—I'm not sure," she said.

Siroy always made Van Sant defensive. He'd made no secret of his disapproval of the way the REACH program was being managed, and of the parallel approach in particular. She knew that this viewpoint would figure in his forthcoming report. Fortunately, he was an overly meticulous writer, so the draft was taking forever. She asked him how the writing was going.

"Slow," he said, shaking his head. "But we do have a title: 'The Rush to Failure.'"

This gave her a start. "What failure?" she asked. "REACH is about to perform a critical repair task."

He shot her a skeptical look. "Rapid ramp-up was a laudable goal," he said. "But you have to give a contractor adequate time for QA. And you have to have a contract that gets the incentives right."

He continued: "We did an analysis. Your compressed schedule forces Hollenbeck-Eskina to cut corners, resulting in prototypes that fail. Substituting computer simulations for rigorous ground testing is a recipe for disaster. There isn't an electronic data management system that would allow the contractors and the CAA to access current test data for analysis. The prototypes aren't equipped with the instruments that would provide adequate test data. And the contractors have no incentive to push back: The cost-plus contract puts all the risk on the CAA. The agency and the contractors have different goals and objectives."

Van Sant couldn't disagree about the contract; its weaknesses had become increasingly evident to her. But if speed was the priority, they were unavoidable. "The contract language is ancient history," she said dismissively.

"You can rewrite history," Siroy said. "Any contract can be altered as long as both sides agree—you know that."

Suddenly, Van Sant saw, one of the staff members who'd been monitoring the goings-on at the space station began ushering MacDonagle away from the reporters, who, smelling blood, tried to follow. MacDonagle caught her eye, and Van Sant didn't like the look she saw on his face. Something bad had happened.

She slipped inside the communications room, where journalists weren't allowed, just before the door was shut. Over the speakers she could hear the astronauts at the space station talking about the power switching unit and using the word "failure." She heard someone say, "We have to go to Plan B."

REACH was probably experiencing the same problem that had come up during its last on-ground test. A system failure notification had gone off, but the contractors had dismissed it as a "reporting error," meaning it hadn't reflected a true mechanical breakdown. Still, no one wanted to deploy REACH while red lights were flashing. There was too great a risk that the robotic arms would fail at a critical moment.

"What's Plan B?" Van Sant asked MacDonagle.

"I don't know," he said quietly, "but whatever it is, it won't involve anything that came from us. REACH is Canada's only contribution to the space station."

Support from on High

"We've got video!" someone shouted, and there on the screens were multiple images of a man in a space suit dangling at the end of a loading crane.

It was well past midnight, but the reporters were still at CAA headquarters. They gathered around the screens. MacDonagle and Van Sant had long since given up trying to avoid them and were mingling with them as the repair attempt unfolded high above West Africa.

Everyone watched in silence as the crane, jury-rigged for the purpose, carried a spacewalker toward the space station's torn solar array. REACH couldn't even be seen—it was docked somewhere else.

"Harris Webb," MacDonagle said ruefully as he watched the figure in the shiny suit. "It's so fitting." Years ago, MacDonagle and Webb had been pilots on the same shuttle mission, and Webb, though much younger, had been chosen to lead it. A U.S. physician, mountaineer, author, pilot, and gourmet cook, as well as an astronaut, he was the ultimate go-to guy, brilliant and fearless—almost to the point of being foolhardy.

The reporters were excitedly discussing his stunt. Because REACH had failed, Webb was going out on the end of the crane to repair the array by hand. In one gloved hand he held what looked like an oversized hockey stick wrapped in insulation, so that he could stop himself from bumping into the arrays. In the other he carried several two-meter lengths of plastic cable that would be used to "stitch" the pliable solar array back together.

"Wow," a reporter gasped as Webb, reaching awkwardly, began threading one of the cables through the openings in the array.

"Cowboy," MacDonagle hissed under his breath. He put his hands on his head and looked at the ceiling.

Van Sant spotted Charlie Truss, one of the reps from Hollenbeck, sitting in a corner, his tie loose. He looked miserable. But she didn't feel pity for him—just annoyance. She went over to him.

"Whatever happens up there tonight," she said, "things are going to change down here. Our only way forward from this fiasco is to show that we've taken concrete steps to improve QA and finally get some positive results."

"I'm all for that," Truss said. "But anything you do to increase QA is going to slow things down. Once that happens, the costs start increasing and you become vulnerable to budget cuts. If we turn our existing contract into a traditional aerospace contract with all those sequential steps and inevitable delays, we might as well say good-bye to the improvements to REACH that are in the pipeline."

"If speed has to be sacrificed for a more reliable REACH, then so be it," Van Sant said. "The contract has major flaws. You're accountable for speed but not performance. We have to share the risk. We need a contract with performance-based incentives and penalties so that we can balance speed, quality, and results. Our goal is reliable components and systems that perform— and that should be your goal, too. We need to work as a unified team willing to push back on each other to get results."

Behind her the reporters gasped. She rushed to a screen and was relieved to see only that Webb, as he had finished his repair, had accidentally let go of a set of pliers, which was now drifting off into space.

But then Webb did something incredible. He turned to his Earth audience and began making a statement defending the failed REACH. "Everyone's going to blame REACH, but they shouldn't," he said. "It's a great piece of technology. I want to commend David MacDonagle and the CAA for overcoming a lot of technical obstacles in a big hurry and getting REACH up here on time. It's going to be a vital part of our operations. One little power-unit problem doesn't mean anything. Complex machines fail—that's just the way it is. We'll fix it, just like we fixed the solar array. I understand that the CAA has a great upgrade coming in the next couple of months—a new set of robot hands that are so nimble they can peel a hard-boiled egg. I say, Get it ready and shoot it up here. We'll start using it right away. I've got a few eggs that need peeling."

Van Sant was stunned, and she could see that Truss was, too. Then, giving her a small smile, he asked: "What were you saying about the contract?"

———————

Tom Cross is a senior director in executive education at the University of Virginia's Darden School of Business, where he develops executive-learning programs for Department of Defense leaders. Previously he was a senior executive at such firms as KFC and Office Depot.

Should Van Sant push for a renegotiated contract for REACH?

See commentaries that follow.

Commentary #1

by Gary L. Moe

Whenever you hear about large, complex, costly government-sponsored tech initiatives that fail to meet expectations, the blame almost always falls on the "hurry up" schedule. If only the public agency hadn't pushed the contractors so hard, if only the developers had been given more time to refine the design, if only a few more months or years had been built into the production schedule, the technology would have worked perfectly. But it's not true.

Government sponsors can give contractors all the time and money in the world to complete a detailed requirements analysis and perfect a project design, and the finished product still probably won't work flawlessly. So-called big-bang design, in which developers labor mightily to get every last detail correct, is incapable of yielding a fully functioning, error-free product, because human beings, no matter how brilliant they are, cannot foresee all the issues that might arise in a complex technology.

What's needed instead is an iterative development process, whereby you build a prototype or even a fully fledged product and then put it out there, test it, and learn from its weaknesses, most of which you couldn't have seen on the drawing board or in a 3-D simulation. In the next iteration, you enhance the product. Then you run another round and another and another until finally you have something that works. The more complex a technology is, the more iterative the development needs to be.

This is how products are developed in the nongovernment sector. Take the auto industry. Cars are so complex that a manufacturer will put a model through a number of builds and a lot of testing before starting full production. In software, this process is called *agile development*. Developers write code for a week, test it to find out how to improve it, and then write some more code.

An interactive approach also works best when it comes to organizational change. No matter how hard you work on designing a reorganization, you will get it only 60% right, so you have to keep working at it, and finally you'll get to 90% right. (It never gets any better than that.)

Iterative development can work both for big long-term projects and for big one-offs, which is what many components of the International Space Station are. You break the development into pieces and apply the build-test, build-test method to the parts.

So why do government organizations, especially those that are defense- or space-related, favor the big-bang approach? There are a number of reasons, some involving the way procurement is handled. But the root of the problem is that iterative development entails experimentation, and experimentation entails failure. Government agencies don't like failure because it ruins political careers. So they try to avoid experimentation. But usually what they end up with is an even bigger failure—and no clue about why it happened.

My advice for Samantha Van Sant, then, is to restructure the contract to break further development of REACH into small chunks and require the contractors to practice iterative improvement, instead of striving for full initial functionality. Cutting down on the functionality delivered in each phase might help too, since 80% of cost and schedule overruns are usually due to the last 10% to 20% of requested functionality.

Gary L. Moe is a director in McKinsey's Business Technology Office and is based in Silicon Valley.

Commentary #2

by Tom Quinly

In the world of cutting-edge product development, the struggle between speed and quality is over. Speed has won—decisively. In today's highly competitive global markets, getting innovations out quickly can mean the difference between success and failure. But it's also a given that the quality must be high. Quality has become table stakes.

A lot of research has been published on the holy grail of lightning-speed development. Concurrent engineering programs, agile teams, risk mitigation programs, spiral development, outsourcing, harmonizing tools, and advanced simulation and modeling tools all can help you attain it, but your own people, processes, and market demands will determine the right recipe. What works best for us is forming small, seasoned, highly talented teams; being clear about time-to-market expectations; making sure developers have the right set of tools; and keeping our technical teams engaged, customer focused, and happy.

Bureaucracy, however, is an innovation killer. It's inevitable that as a business grows, things that don't add value creep into processes. With each slipup there's a tendency to add another process check. In isolation, each makes perfect sense, but in the aggregate, innovation is choked, and the team can't move nimbly.

I recall an experience early in my career, when a major development project had gone poorly. At an executive review, I was prepared to explain what had happened, what we'd learned, and what we'd done to stop the bleeding. Our CEO looked around at the others in attendance and said that he was disappointed—not in the group that had failed (mine), but in the other groups, because they *hadn't* failed. They weren't being as aggressive as he expected. That story lives on in the lore of the company, and it says a lot about our culture.

It's not that we encourage failure—we use it as a tool. Complex development programs rarely (if ever) come out of the gate perfectly; something unanticipated often happens. A lot can be learned from reviewing failures and looking at processes, expectations, people, and tools. Were our requirements too ambitious or ill defined? Did we not map the highest-risk areas and have well-designed mitigation plans? This relentless focus on learning improves predictability, reduces cycle time, and helps us get a high-quality offering to market ahead of the competition.

That's why I would advise Van Sant to give up the dinosaur perspective that speed means having to sacrifice quality. She should engage the entire team in examining the failures and exploring ways to achieve quality without upsetting the schedule. If REACH has few qualified alternative partners, then disrupting a long-standing contract with a highly experienced and specialized partner would be counterproductive. If Hollenbeck-Eskina is the best option, I would avoid having to reopen the contract and potentially lose the partner's deep project knowledge. However, if Hollenbeck-Eskina was not totally engaged and forthcoming in helping understand and correct the failures, it may be time to involve other potential partners or to stand firm on a contract renegotiation.

Tom Quinly is president of the motion control segment at Curtiss-Wright Controls, based in Charlotte, North Carolina, which develops products for aerospace, defense, and industrial markets.

Chapter 11
Getting Your Project Off on the Right Foot

With your project team formed, your charter delivered, and the team's tasks scheduled, you've still got a few critical matters to take care of before work commences. First, your project needs a **launch**—a special event that marks its official beginning. Second, you must set up activities and provide tools that foster team building. And third, you must institute behavioral norms that make collaborative work possible and communicate them to all participants.

Why Launch Meetings Matter

The launch represents the very first project milestone. If conducted properly, it has substantial symbolic value.

The best way to kick off a project is through an all-team meeting, one with appropriate levels of gravity and

Adapted from *Harvard Business Essentials: Managing Projects Large and Small* (product #6280BC), Harvard Business Review Press, 2004

fanfare. You'll have already held many planning sessions with key individuals—but those informal get-togethers are no substitute for a face-to-face meeting attended by all team members, the sponsor, your stakeholders, and, if appropriate, the organization's highest-ranking official.

Physical presence at this meeting has great psychological significance, particularly for geographically dispersed teams, whose members may have few future opportunities to convene as a group. Being together at the beginning of their long journey and getting to know one another on a personal level will build commitment and bolster participants' sense that this team and project are important. If certain people cannot attend the launch meeting because of their geographic location, they should participate virtually, through videoconferencing or, at the very least, speakerphone.

The sponsor's presence and demeanor at the launch speak volumes about the importance—or unimportance—ascribed to the project's mission. As Jon Katzenbach and Douglas Smith write in "The Discipline of Teams" (HBR March–April 1993):

> *When potential teams first gather, everyone monitors the signals given by others to confirm, suspend, or dispel assumptions and concerns. They pay particular attention to those in authority: the team leader and any executives who set up, oversee, or otherwise influence the team. And, as always, what such leaders do is more important than what they say. If a senior executive leaves the team kickoff to take a phone call ten minutes*

after the session has begun and he never returns, people get the message.

Here are your main tasks for the launch:

- **Welcome everyone aboard.** Acknowledge and thank all those who will contribute to the project. Mention each person by name. Many attendees will be core team members, and others will be peripheral members who participate for a limited time or in a limited way. But all are members.

- **Ask your sponsor to say a few words.** Have him articulate *why* the project's work is important and *how* its goals are aligned with larger organizational objectives. Otherwise, people won't see consequences for themselves and the company, and they won't make their best effort.

- **Make introductions.** Unless people are already familiar with one another, they probably won't know who has which skills. If the group isn't too large, ask participants to introduce themselves, to say something about their background and expertise, and to explain what they hope to contribute to and get from the project.

- **Share the charter.** Explain the goals, deliverables, and timetables you've documented.

- **Seek consensus.** Get everyone to agree on what the charter means.

- **Describe the resources available.** Although you'll certainly want to stoke the team's enthusiasm at the launch, it's equally important to set realistic expectations about the amount of support (both workers and budget) you'll have.

- **Describe incentives.** What will members receive, beyond their normal compensation, if the team meets or exceeds its goals?

Though participants will develop a sense of belonging and common goals only with time and through shared experiences, you'll have planted the seeds at the launch meeting. People should now begin to think of themselves as members of a real team.

Provide Activities and Tools for Working Together

Giving people collective goals and handing out free T-shirts with a team logo creates a team in name only. Project teams gel through joint work, idea sharing, and give-and-take in decision making and information exchange.

A project manager can facilitate that kind of collaboration through regularly scheduled meetings, communication tools such as project newsletters and websites, and the physical colocation of team members. Off-site social events may also be valuable, since they can help groups cohere. You'll want to encourage people to forge the bonds of trust and friendship that make team-based work stimulating and productive.

Establish Norms of Behavior

It takes time to build an effective project team. Individuals come to the effort with personal agendas. Some may view their new teammates as competitors for promotions, recognition, and rewards. Others may harbor grudges against one or more of those with whom they have been thrown together. And there's always a member or two lacking in social skills.

Such problems can undermine your project if they're not contained or neutralized. One of the best ways to manage them is to set up unambiguous norms of behavior that apply equally to all. As Jon Katzenbach and Douglas Smith point out in *The Wisdom of Teams*, the most critical rules pertain to:

- **Attendance.** The team cannot make decisions and accomplish its work if members fail to show up for meetings or joint work sessions. If you, the leader, are chronically late or absent, people will follow your example.

- **Interruptions.** Turn cell phones off during meetings and work sessions. Also, make it clear that people are not to interrupt others. Everyone has a right to speak.

- **Sacred cows.** Agree that no issues will be off-limits. For example, if a process-reengineering team knows that a change will upset a particular executive, its members should not be reluctant to discuss it.

- **Disagreements.** Team players are bound to come up with competing solutions as they tackle problems. Encourage them to vent disagreements in constructive ways.

- **Confidentiality.** Some team issues may be sensitive. Members will discuss them freely only if what is said within the team stays within the team.

- **Action orientation.** The purpose of teams is not to meet and discuss. It's to act and produce results. Make that clear from the beginning.

What behavioral norms should your group observe? That depends on the purpose of the group and the personalities of its members. But the basics include mutual respect, a commitment to active listening, and an understanding of how to voice concerns and handle conflict.

To guarantee the free flow of ideas, some groups may want to adopt specific guidelines that support calculated risk taking, for instance, or spell out procedures for acknowledging and handling failure. Whatever norms your group follows, make sure all members have a hand in establishing them—and that everyone agrees to abide by them. Members' participation and acceptance will head off many future problems.

Chapter 12
The Discipline of Teams

A summary of the full-length HBR article by **Jon R. Katzenbach** *and* **Douglas K. Smith,** *highlighting key ideas.*

THE IDEA IN BRIEF

The word *team* gets bandied about so loosely that many managers are oblivious to its real meaning—or its true potential. With a run-of-the-mill working group, performance is a function of what the members do as individuals. A team's performance, by contrast, calls for both individual and mutual accountability.

Though it may not seem like anything special, mutual accountability can lead to astonishing results. It enables a team to achieve performance levels that are far greater than the individual bests of the team's members.

Excerpted from Harvard Business Review, July–August 2005 (republished from 1993), Reprint #R0507P. To buy the full-length article, visit www.hbr.org.

To achieve these benefits, team members must do more than listen, respond constructively, and provide support to one another. In addition to sharing these team-building values, they must share an essential *discipline*.

THE IDEA IN PRACTICE

A team's essential discipline comprises five characteristics:

1. **A meaningful common purpose that the team has helped shape.** Most teams are responding to an initial mandate from outside the team. But to be successful, the team must "own" this purpose, develop its own spin on it.

2. **Specific performance goals that flow from the common purpose.** For example, getting a new product to market in less than half the normal time. Compelling goals inspire and challenge a team, give it a sense of urgency. They also have a leveling effect, requiring members to focus on the collective effort necessary rather than any differences in title or status.

3. **A mix of complementary skills.** These include technical or functional expertise, problem-solving and decision-making skills, and interpersonal skills. Successful teams rarely have all the needed skills at the outset—they develop them as they learn what the challenge requires.

4. **A strong commitment to how the work gets done.** Teams must agree on who will do what jobs, how schedules will be established and honored, and how decisions will be made and modified. On a genuine team, each member does equivalent amounts of real work; all members, the leader included, contribute in concrete ways to the team's collective work-products.

5. **Mutual accountability.** Trust and commitment cannot be coerced. The process of agreeing upon appropriate goals serves as the crucible in which members forge their accountability to each other—not just to the leader.

Once the essential discipline has been established, a team is free to concentrate on the critical challenges it faces:

- For a team whose purpose is to make recommendations, that means making a fast and constructive start and providing a clean handoff to those who will implement the recommendations.

- For a team that makes or does things, it's keeping the specific performance goals in sharp focus.

- For a team that runs things, the primary task is distinguishing the challenges that require a real team approach from those that don't.

If a task doesn't demand joint work-products, a working group can be the more effective option. Team opportunities are usually those in which hierarchy or organizational boundaries inhibit the skills and perspectives needed for optimal results. Little wonder, then, that teams have become the primary units of productivity in high-performance organizations.

———

Jon R. Katzenbach is a senior partner at Booz & Company and a former director of McKinsey & Company. **Douglas K. Smith** is an organizational consultant and a former partner at McKinsey & Company.

Phase 3
Implementation

Chapter 13
Effective Project Meetings

Run your meetings well, and you'll infuse your project with energy, momentum, and direction. How do you make them productive? Follow these simple guidelines.

Setting the Stage for the Meeting

- Make sure a meeting is even necessary. If you can accomplish your goal efficiently without calling one (via e-mail, for example), do so—and avoid eating up everyone's time.

- Clarify the meeting's objective. If it is to make a decision, explain that and give participants the time and materials needed to prepare.

- Sound out key participants on important agenda items ahead of time. What you discover may suggest that alterations are in order.

Adapted from *Harvard Business Essentials: Managing Projects Large and Small* (product #6198BC), Harvard Business Review Press, 2004, and Harvard ManageMentor, an online product of Harvard Business Publishing

- Invite only people who have something to contribute or who can learn from the discussion.

- Provide an agenda in advance that clearly supports the objective.

- Insist that people get up to speed on the issues before they arrive, bring relevant materials with them, and show up ready to contribute to the discussion.

Running the Meeting

- Restate the meeting's purpose. This will sharpen the group's focus.

- Let everyone have a say. If one or two individuals are dominating the conversation or if certain attendees are shy about leaping in, say, "Thanks for those ideas, Phil. What are your thoughts about this problem, Charlotte?"

- Keep the discussion centered on the key issues.

- End with confirmation and an action plan that includes a clear time frame: "OK, we've decided to hire DataWhack to install the new servers. And, as agreed, I will obtain the purchase order today, Bill will phone the salesperson later this week and set up the schedule, and Janet will begin looking for someone to take the old equipment off our hands. We'll regroup at the usual time next week to see where things stand."

Following Up

- Send out a note summarizing the meeting's outcomes. People will be encouraged by it because it's evidence that the team is one step closer to its goal.

- Remind individuals of their tasks and deadlines.

- Offer support to anyone who may be overwhelmed with other work or may struggle with a task. People are often reluctant to ask for assistance, even when they recognize that they need it.

Chapter 14
The Adaptive Approach to Project Management

Does your project involve an unfamiliar technology or material? Is it substantially larger than others you've overseen? Are the tasks different from those your team has handled in the past?

If you answered yes to one or more of those questions, the traditional approach to project management may not work. That's because it takes for granted that you can pinpoint what needs to be done, what it will cost, and how much time you'll need. In situations with higher levels of uncertainty—if you face unanticipated risks,

Adapted from "Project Adaptation: Dealing with What You Cannot Anticipate," *Harvard Business Essentials: Managing Projects Large and Small* (product #6273BC), Harvard Business Review Press, 2004

A NEW MODEL FOR SPONSORS

The adaptive model of project management creates a new role for project sponsors, one that Robert Austin likened to venture capitalism in the 2002 *Science* article "Project Management and Discovery." Rather than give teams a big pile of resources at the beginning, they support projects in stages, as results roll in. Like VCs, sponsors advance resources to purchase information and reduce uncertainty—and each investment gives them the option of remaining in the game.

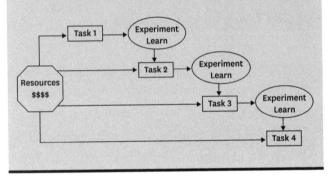

for instance, or if the range of potential outcomes is very wide—decision tools such as return on investment, net present value, and internal rate of return (which assume predictability of future cash flows) cease to be useful. You may have to consider a more adaptive approach.

In their research on large IT implementation projects, Lynda Applegate, Robert Austin, and Warren McFarlan (the authors of *Corporate Information Strategy and Management*) found that companies such as Cisco Systems have enjoyed success with adaptive project-management models that:

- **Approach tasks iteratively.** Teams engage in small incremental tasks, evaluate the outcomes of those tasks, and make adjustments as they move forward.

- **Have fast cycles.** Short lead times allow an iterative approach.

- **Emphasize early value delivery.** Small, early deliverables encourage feedback and the incorporation of learning into subsequent activities.

- **Staff the project with people who can adapt.** Some people are faster learners than others and are more amenable to change.

Cisco refers to its approach as "rapid iterative prototyping." Many tasks serve as probes—that is, as learning experiences for later steps. This tactic is analogous to the notion of the "cheap kills" that research and development organizations use to sort through many possibilities quickly and at low cost. When the right solution is not apparent, they try a number of simple experiments to separate promising and unpromising options. Even failed experiments provide insights into what will work.

WHAT-IF PLANNING AND CHUNKING

To enhance their ability to adapt to shifting conditions, some firms rely on the techniques that Cathleen Benko and F. Warren McFarlan call "what-if planning and chunking" in their book *Connecting the Dots: Aligning Projects with Objectives in Unpredictable Times.* Sweden-based software firm Ellipsus Systems used **what-if planning** to decide which programming standard—wireless application protocol (WAP) or Java—it would choose for its software. Since it was unclear which standard would dominate, cofounder Rikard Kjellberg designed projects based on both and then took early prototypes to a trade show to test participants' preferences. His contingency planning led to a successful partnership with Java-maker Sun Microsystems.

Minnesota hotel-management company Carlson Hospitality Worldwide uses **chunking** to break big, expensive projects into smaller, more manageable ones, thereby boosting their chances of receiving approval and funding. After the board of directors rejected a $15 million request to overhaul the company's central reservation system, managers broke the project into work units that each had stand-alone benefits and minimal mutual dependencies. That is, if one chunk was canceled, others could still move ahead. The board soon approved the first chunk. Ultimately, Carlson's new reservation system was voted best in the industry; its voice-reservation chunk alone generated $40 million in annual revenue by 2003. "Chunking helps us learn constantly and perpetually reassess our priorities," says CIO Scott Heintzeman. "It also reduces risk and focuses people's efforts on each work unit. And because the work on each chunk extends for no more than three to six months, people maintain their energy and enthusiasm."

Adapted from "Close the Gap Between Projects and Strategy," *Harvard Management Update* (product #U0406A), June 2004

Chapter 15
Why Good Projects Fail Anyway

A summary of the full-length HBR article by **Nadim F. Matta** *and* **Ronald N. Ashkenas,** *highlighting key ideas.*

THE IDEA IN BRIEF

Big projects fail at an astonishing rate—well over half, by some estimates. Why are efforts involving many people working over extended periods of time so problematic? Traditional project planning carries three serious risks:

- **White space:** Planners leave gaps in the project plan by failing to anticipate all the project's required activities and work streams.

- **Execution:** Project team members fail to carry out designated activities properly.

Excerpted from Harvard Business Review, September 2003, reprint #R0309H. To buy the full-length article, visit www.hbr.org.

- **Integration:** Team members execute all tasks flawlessly—on time and within budget—but don't knit all the project pieces together at the end. The project doesn't deliver the intended results.

Manage these risks with **rapid-results initiatives**: small projects designed to quickly deliver mini-versions of the big project's end results. Through rapid-results initiatives, project team members iron out kinks early and on a small scale. Rapid-results teams serve as models for subsequent teams who can roll out the initiative on a larger scale with greater confidence. The teams feel the satisfaction of delivering real value, and their company gets early payback on its investments.

THE IDEA IN PRACTICE

Rapid-results initiatives have several defining characteristics:

- **Results oriented:** The initiatives produce measurable payoffs on a small scale.

  Example: The World Bank wanted to improve the productivity of 120,000 small-scale farmers in Nicaragua by 30% in 16 years. Its rapid-results initiatives included "increase pig weight on 30 farms by 30% in 100 days using enhanced corn seed."

- **Vertical:** The initiatives include people from different parts of the organization—or even different organizations—who work in tandem within a very short time frame to implement slices of several horizontal—or parallel-track—activities. The traditional emphasis on disintegrated, horizontal, long-term activities gives way to the integrated, vertical, and short-term. The teams uncover activities falling in the white space between horizontal project streams, and properly integrate *all* the activities.

> *Example:* Take a companywide CRM project. Traditionally, one team might analyze customers, another select the software, a third develop training programs. When the project's finally complete, though, it may turn out that the salespeople won't enter the requisite data because they don't understand why they need to. Using rapid-results initiatives, a single team might be charged with increasing the revenues of one sales group in one region within four months. To reach that goal, team members would have to draw on the work of all the parallel teams. And they would quickly discover the salespeople's resistance and other unforeseen issues.

- **Fast:** The initiatives strive for results and lessons in less than 100 days. Designed to deliver quick wins, they more importantly change the way teams work. How? The short time frame establishes a sense of urgency from the start, poses personal challenges, and leaves no time to waste on inter-organizational bickering. It also stimulates creativity and encourages team members to experiment with new ideas that deliver concrete results.

Balancing Vertical and Horizontal Activities

Vertical, rapid-results initiatives offer many benefits. But that doesn't mean you should eliminate all horizontal activities. Such activities offer cost-effective economies of scale. The key is to *balance* vertical and horizontal, spread insights among teams, and blend all activities into an overall implementation strategy.

> *Example:* Dissatisfied with its 8% revenue increase in two years, office-products company Avery Dennison launched 15 rapid-results teams in three North American divisions. After only three months, the teams were meeting their goals—e.g., securing one new order for an enhanced product with one large customer within 100 days. Top management extended the rapid-results process throughout the company, reinforcing it with an extensive employee communication program. As horizontal activities continued, dozens more teams started rapid-results initiatives. Results? $8 million+ in new sales, and $50 million in sales forecast by year-end.

————————

Nadim F. Matta is a managing partner, and **Ronald N. Ashkenas** is a senior partner, of Schaffer Consulting in Stamford, Connecticut.

Chapter 16
Monitoring and Controlling Your Project

by Ray Sheen

Unlike processes—where the same people repeatedly perform the same activities—projects often involve unique activities (such as using new technologies, building new buildings, or writing new software) carried out by individuals who may be working together for the first time. So as a project leader, you'll need to actively monitor progress to figure out whether your plan is really bringing the team closer to its objectives.

When monitoring and controlling a project, you'll follow five basic steps:

1. Track project activities

It's important to check in with team members regularly to make sure they're completing their tasks and meeting quality standards. You can do this most effectively through team meetings if everyone works at the same location. However, given how common distributed teams are in today's business environment, it can be difficult to get the entire group together. When that's the case, I conduct separate working sessions with individuals or small groups needed for particular activities. For example, I recently participated in a "live meeting" conference call where engineers from three locations helped prepare a product-development proposal for a customer. If I had created a draft, sent it around for comments, and then tried to integrate all the feedback, it could easily have taken weeks to complete the document. Instead, I had the right engineers reviewing it over the phone for about three hours, until everybody agreed on the wording. After a working session like this, I loop the rest of the team in at a larger group meeting or through e-mail.

I also use "buddy checks" to verify that tasks are done properly. When someone completes an activity, another team member looks at the results. This is not an in-depth technical analysis; it's a quick check to confirm that the person who did the work hasn't accidentally overlooked something or misunderstood the requirements. A team member checking a training plan for a new system, for example, would make certain that all departments in need of training have been included. If possible, have someone who will *use* the results of the activity do the buddy check. When I worked with a medical device company on developing a new product, I had its regulatory department review the design documentation and test data to flag any missing information that would be required later for regulatory submittal. If a team member with a stake in the activity's result is not available, you can do the buddy check yourself—but make it clear that it's not a performance appraisal. It's just one team member looking out for another.

2. Collect performance data

A few companies have project management information systems that automatically generate reports. If you have access to one, by all means use it—but also seek out performance data through short **pulse meetings,** where team members share status updates on activities and assess risks, either face-to-face or virtually. I limit these to 10 minutes and discuss only the tasks started or finished since the last meeting. The purpose is to get a quick sense of where things are, not to roll up sleeves. If the team identifies any problems or risks, I resolve them in a separate working session with the appropriate individuals.

I normally pulse projects on a weekly basis, which allows me to track progress adequately and identify problems in time to respond to them. However, when a project is in crisis mode, the "pulse rate" quickens. I once managed a project in which the power system for a new facility failed three days before the building needed to be up and running. An important business objective hinged on that deadline. The team worked around the clock to identify the cause of the failure, replace the destroyed component, and bring the facility back on line. All that would normally have taken two to three months, but we had three days, so I pulsed the project every three hours.

3. Analyze performance to determine whether the plan still holds

Activities seldom go precisely as anticipated. They may take more or less time; they may overrun or underrun the budget. A departure from your plan isn't a problem unless it's likely to compromise the team's objectives. On one project, I had an engineer report at a pulse meeting that a new mold would be two weeks late. But since the mold wasn't on our critical path and we had nearly six weeks of slack time in that portion of the schedule, the team didn't need to take special action. If the late deliverable had put us in danger of missing an important goal, I would have called a meeting with the appropriate team members to figure out a solution.

This is the time when careful project planning pays dividends. Knowing the critical path will help you decide which issues warrant a schedule change. If you've identified risks up front that could undermine your objectives, you can more easily recognize which snags are threats to the project's success. Having estimated each activity's duration and costs and carefully noted any uncertainties, you'll be able to distinguish between variances that aren't a big deal and those that suggest larger underlying problems.

When a plan does need revising, you may have to extend the end date, apply budget reserves, remove deliverables from the project's scope, or even cancel the project. On one software development project I oversaw, we had an excessively "buggy" first release. Before trying to fix the software, I quickly checked the requirements document and realized that the developers were using an out-of-date version. We had to reschedule the software development task for that module, causing us to delay project completion by about a month, but the change clearly needed to be made.

4. Report progress to your stakeholders

Some project managers and team members perceive **stakeholder reviews**—which involve preparing reports and conducting progress meetings—as wasted effort because they take time away from other activities. However, if managed properly, these reviews propel a project toward success. There are three types: management reviews, tollgate reviews, and technical reviews. For all three, record and circulate action items, and keep meeting minutes in the project file for future reference.

The purpose of the **management review** is to manage risk. Stakeholders may examine several projects at a time to see if the portfolio as a whole will generate the desired business performance and to identify systemic weaknesses. They'll look at individual projects on their own merits as well. Such reviews are normally held at regular intervals—monthly, for instance. When conducting them, keep in mind that your stakeholders care about reaching business goals, not about following the team's day-to-day activities. I recently attended a review where the project leader spent nearly 30 minutes describing technical designs the team was considering and testing, which only bored and frustrated the stakeholders. Instead, he should have spent five minutes telling them the project was on schedule (it was), that the team had made progress on its technical analysis (it had), and that no new risks had been identified.

Creating a **project dashboard** is a great way to summarize your objectives and show stakeholders whether the project, as currently planned and managed, will achieve them. (You can break it down into components such as schedule, cost, and performance.) This is often called a **stoplight chart,** since it usually indicates activity statuses in red, yellow, and green. Most companies have a standard format to help senior managers quickly and efficiently assess progress and risks on many projects. When using color coding, make sure everyone understands exactly what each color means. For example, do you list all incomplete tasks in red? Or are some of them green, because the plan for completion is approved and under way?

When you need to report bad news in a management review, always couch it in terms of risks to project objectives. Explain how certain task delays will prevent the team from realizing project goals on time, for instance, or how a resource shortage will reduce the rigor of an activity and thus the quality of its deliverable. When you present problems, also give options for responding to them and discuss the risks associated with each solution. The stakeholders will decide which risks they want the business to take.

The **tollgate review** (also called the **stage-gate review,** or **phase-gate review**) is a decision meeting, not a status check. It's used when a business plans and executes projects in discrete phases. In it, the project team summarizes the results of the preceding phase and presents a plan for the next phase. The stakeholders assess the plan, options, and risks, and then decide whether to approve, redirect, or cancel the project. If they say to proceed to the next phase, they also provide the team with the necessary resources, including funding.

At a **technical review** (sometimes referred to as a **peer review**), an independent team of experts—internal or external consultants, say, or representatives from a regulatory agency—provides an in-depth analysis of project results. The purpose is to ensure that team members did the work accurately, completely, and to the right quality standard. Stakeholders may give a stamp of approval at this time: If the team has successfully completed one phase of the project, it can now proceed to a tollgate review for approval to begin the next phase.

5. Manage changes to the plan

When revising a plan, you may make major changes or just minor tweaks that will allow the team to meet its objectives.

If you propose major changes to your stakeholders, spell out the costs and risks of adopting them and those of sticking with the original plan. A defense contractor that I work with was asked by the Air Force to improve performance of a weapon-system component. After the Air Force reviewed the proposed options (which included costs, risks, and schedules) and selected one, the contractor synchronized updates to design documentation, manufacturing processes, supplier contracts, the project schedule, and the budget so the transition would be as seamless as possible. When making such large-scale revisions, record them (along with the rationale) on some type of change log in the project records. You can use your normal project-planning processes and techniques to revise your plan. Send the new plan to your team members, and explain any changes that affect them.

Minor changes may come up as you're implementing a contingency plan or working out details of a portion of the project that was planned only at a high level. The project team can usually manage these on its own, without seeking stakeholder approval, unless the changes will directly affect stakeholders or their departments.

As you're monitoring your project, remember that meeting your objectives trumps everything else. Don't get hung up on compliance with the original plan. In my experience, almost every project plan must be revised at some point—especially when you're developing new products or systems, because what you learn in the early stages sheds light on how later-stage tasks should take shape. Don't be afraid to change course if it will bring you within reach of your goals.

———————

Ray Sheen teaches and consults on project and process management. He has more than 25 years of experience leading projects in defense, product development, manufacturing, IT, and other areas, and has run a project management office in GE's Electrical Distribution business.

Chapter 17
Managing People Problems on Your Team

Your most important resource is your people. After you've done the hard work of selecting the right team members and getting them revved up for the project, you need to make sure they stay on task, pull their weight, work collaboratively, and reach the quality standards you've established with your stakeholders. If you don't, you're highly unlikely to meet your goals, let alone your deadlines and budget targets. Here's how to recognize and deal with various people problems you may encounter as a project manager.

Adapted from *Pocket Mentor: Managing Projects* (product #1878), Harvard Business Review Press, 2006

Implementation

Team structure problems

Problem	Possible causes	Potential impact	Recommended action
• Your team lacks necessary skills.	• You overlooked certain skill requirements during planning. • You discovered a need for new skills in the midst of the project.	• The project doesn't move forward as fast as it should, or it stalls.	• Arrange for a team member to be trained in the skills needed. • Hire outside consultants or contractors who have the skills.

Problem	Possible causes	Potential impact	Recommended action
• A team member leaves.	• This could happen for many reasons, ranging from sudden illness to departure from the organization.	• Severity depends on the skills and knowledge lost: • If you can easily redistribute the work or hire someone with the same expertise, the impact may be slight. • If not, the loss could create a crisis.	• Have backup team members at the ready. • Cross-train people so they can fill in for one another. • Make one person's departure an opportunity to bring an even more skilled team member on board.

Interpersonal problems

Problem	Possible causes	Potential impact	Recommended action
• Team members are *too* friendly.	• They spend excessive amounts of time chatting or discussing personal problems.	• Overall productivity decreases. • Time is wasted, and the project slows down. • Hard-working team members resent those who work less efficiently.	• Emphasize that social gatherings need to be planned for after work. • Reorganize team subgroups to disrupt cliques.
Problem	**Possible causes**	**Potential impact**	**Recommended action**
• Conflicts exist within the team.	• People have a hard time reconciling different personalities, working styles, or areas of expertise.	• The schedule, quality of work, overall productivity, and team cohesiveness could all suffer.	• Focus team members on the project's goals, not on personal feelings. • Separate the underlying causes from the surface disturbances, so you can solve problems at the root. • Propose solutions, not blame.

(continued)

Productivity problems (continued)

Problem	Possible causes	Potential impact	Recommended action
• Time is spent on the wrong tasks.	• People manage their time poorly. • A team member prefers some tasks over others, regardless of relative importance. • You've sent the wrong message about priorities.	• Work on critical tasks is delayed. • The overall project is delayed.	• Clarify which tasks are most important. • Assign tasks to pairs of team members to work on together so they can keep each other in check. • Provide resources to help members improve time management skills.

Problem	Possible causes	Potential impact	Recommended action
• The quality of the work is poor.	• A team member misunderstands the requirements of the job. • Different people measure the work by different standards. • Someone doesn't have adequate skills to complete a task.	• Work must be redone, costing money and time. • The project fails.	• Be clear from the start about quality expectations and standards of measure. • Develop an action plan for improving the quality of the team member's work. • Provide training and support to develop skills.

Chapter 18
The Tools of Cooperation and Change

A summary of the full-length HBR article by **Clayton M. Christensen, Matt Marx,** *and* **Howard H. Stevenson**, *highlighting key ideas.*

Editor's note: Sometimes you need to manage change within projects. Other times the projects themselves are agents of change in a company, and you have to overcome organizational resistance. Arm yourself with the right tools, and you can elicit cooperation rather than entrenchment.

THE IDEA IN BRIEF

Why do managers struggle so hard to get employees' cooperation on change initiatives? Even charismatic leaders

Excerpted from *Harvard Business Review*, October 2006, reprint #R0610D. To buy the full-length article, visit www.hbr.org.

have spotty records—winning commitment to change in some cases but failing dismally in others.

According to Christensen, Marx, and Stevenson, too many leaders use the wrong change tools at the wrong time—wasting energy and risking their credibility. For example, a vision statement helps get people on board if they already agree on where their organization should go. Without that consensus, vision statements won't change behavior—aside from provoking a collective rolling of eyes.

How to wield the *right* change tools, at the right time? Gauge how strongly your people agree on 1) where they want to go and 2) how to get there. Then select tools based on the nature of employees' agreement. For instance, if people disagree about goals and ways to achieve them (common during mergers), use power tools—such as threatening to make key decisions yourself. If employees have goals that differ from your company's but agree on how work should be done (think independent contractors), use management tools—including training and performance measurement systems.

Choose the correct tools, and you spur the changes your firm needs to stay ahead of rivals.

THE IDEA IN PRACTICE

Selecting the Right Change Tools

Scenario #1: If employees agree on goals but disagree on how to achieve them, use **leadership tools**: vision, charisma, salesmanship, and role modeling.

Example: In December 1995, Microsoft's Bill Gates published his visionary "Internet Tidal Wave" memo. The memo persuaded employees that the World Wide Web would become integral to computing (which countered most employees' beliefs). Employees responded with products that crippled Internet rival Netscape and maintained Microsoft's dominance in the software industry (which employees and the company wanted).

Scenario #2: If employees disagree on both goals and how to get there, use **power tools**: threats, hiring and promotion, control systems, and coercion.

Example: To merge JP Morgan with BankOne, CEO Jamie Dimon slashed hundreds of executives' salaries 20% to 50%. He threatened to select a single IT platform to replace the firm's myriad systems if the IT staff didn't pick one themselves in six weeks. And he told branch managers they'd lose their jobs if they failed to meet sales quotas.

Scenario #3: If employees agree on both goals and how to get there, use **culture tools** to counter complacence. In particular, use "disaggregation" (separating the organization into entities that each have their own agreed-upon goals and plans for achieving them) to disrupt high-level agreement about goals and methods that could otherwise preserve the status quo.

Example: Hewlett-Packard recognized that its new inkjet printer business—with its unique technology and economics—could thrive only if it was protected from the cultural expectations of its traditional laser printing business. Disaggregating the two businesses eliminated the need for cooperation between them and enabled the groups to operate on very different profit models.

Scenario #4: If employees disagree on goals but agree on how work should be done, use **management tools**: measurement systems, standard operating procedures, and training.

Example: In many companies, the reasons unionized manufacturing workers come to work differ markedly from those of senior managers. But as long as workers accept management's assertion that following certain manufacturing procedures will help them make products with desired quality and cost, they will follow those procedures.

Clayton M. Christensen is the Kim B. Clark Professor of Business Administration at Harvard Business School in Boston. **Matt Marx** was a doctoral student at HBS. **Howard H. Stevenson** is HBS's Sarofim-Rock Baker Foundation Professor of Business Administration, Emeritus, and the chairman of the board at Harvard Business Publishing.

Chapter 19
Don't Throw Good Money (or Time) After Bad

by Jimmy Guterman

You approved the development of a high-profile new product for your company a year ago—but now things aren't going well. Despite previous forecasts that customers needed your product, the market has changed, and the response is uncertain at best. But you're not going to give up and throw away $10 million, are you?

Actually, spending another dime on a doomed product is the wrong decision. Yet chasing after **sunk costs** (investments that are no longer recoverable) is a common error. *Just another couple hundred thousand dollars,* you say to yourself, *and we'll be able to recoup our investment.*

Adapted from *Harvard Management Update* (product #U0205D), May 2002

Don't fall for that line of reasoning. True managerial wisdom lies in a kind of forgetfulness—the ability to ignore prior investments, costs, and benefits, and to focus instead on the situation at hand. When faced with insufficient information and tight time constraints, managers regularly use simplifying strategies, known as **judgment heuristics,** as decision-making shortcuts. Problem is, human psychology always enters into the process, leading to cognitive biases—conclusions based on misperceptions or faulty inferences. The sunk-cost trap is a type of cognitive bias. Harvard Business School professor Max H. Bazerman, author of *Judgment in Managerial Decision Making,* likens this "nonrational escalation of commitment" to standing at a bus stop for hour after hour. At some point, you have to admit that the bus is not coming.

You can avoid escalating your company's commitment to a product, person, or strategy beyond a reasonable point. These guidelines will help.

Don't make choices merely to justify past decisions

Should you retain an underperforming, abusive contractor simply because you hired him and don't want to be accused of flip-flopping? Should you continue to extend credit to a company that has consistently failed to meet its obligations, since it promises that just one more loan will turn everything around? In the abstract, the answer to both questions is clearly no. But it's easy to let context obscure your better judgment.

Avoid this problem by gathering external evidence to support your choices. When deciding whether to move forward on a project, consult as many outside sources and devil's advocates as you can, so you're sure to consider how people other than your supervisor might view your quandary. Failure to see the big picture often results in overly cautious decision making, which in turn can lead to the sunk-cost trap.

Focus on the quality of the decision, not the quality of the outcome

Many people fall into the sunk-cost trap because they fear being judged for the unfortunate consequences of their good-at-the-time decisions. When things go sour, HBS professor emeritus Howard Raiffa explains, decision makers become "more worried about acts of commission, like changing course, than acts of omission, like continuing to take the company down the wrong road. *If I just go along as things are now*, the thinking goes, *things might change. If I commit an act of commission and admit that the current course is wrongheaded, that may trigger a review*. . . . There are huge internal and external pressures to keep going even if all parties realize it's wrong and it's going to stay wrong."

If you're managing a decision maker, you can prevent unnecessary escalations of commitment by making it clear that no one will be punished for not owning a crystal ball.

The more you equate time with money, the more susceptible you are to the sunk-cost trap

That's the conclusion Hong Kong University of Science and Technology marketing professor Dilip Soman reached after conducting a series of sunk-cost experiments. As he noted in a 2001 article in the *Journal of Behavioral Decision Making,* sunk costs don't usually trip us up when our main investment is time. But they do present a problem when we become more adept at converting that investment into a monetary equivalent.

Use decision rules to prevent cloudy thinking

In *Judgment in Managerial Decision Making,* Bazerman lays out a common scenario: "You personally decided to hire a new middle-level manager to work for you. Although you had expected excellent performance, early reports suggest that she is not performing as you had hoped. Should you fire her? Perhaps you really can't afford her current level of performance. On the other hand, you have invested a fair amount in her training. Furthermore, she may just be in the process of learning the ropes. So you decide to invest in her a bit longer and provide additional resources so that she can succeed. But still she does not perform as expected. Although you have more reason to 'cut your losses,' you now have even more invested in this employee."

Precise targets can help you avoid such rounds of rationalizing. Establish in advance how much time and money you're willing to pour into a project or person before you need to see specific results. As the investment sage Warren Buffett once said, "When you find yourself in a hole, the best thing you can do is stop digging." Targets tell you when to put down the shovel. They enable you to discriminate, says Bazerman, "between situations in which persistence will pay off and situations in which it will not."

Jimmy Guterman was a senior editor at hbr.org.

Phase 4
Closeout

Chapter 20
Handing Off Authority and Control

by Ray Sheen

Now that you've executed your project, it's time to gauge your success and then finalize activities, ranging from transferring control of new systems or facilities to presenting deliverables to stakeholders. Why not finalize activities first? Because you can't know when to close up shop until you've determined whether you've met your objectives.

In other words, success means achieving the goals in your charter and scope statement—not necessarily finishing all the tasks on your Gantt chart. Whether your team is releasing a product, adopting a new system, opening a facility, or improving a process, you'll need to validate that those goals, if still relevant, have been reached. Since stakeholders care far more about realizing business benefits than they do about adhering to the plan's "critical path," the team needs to get out of the weeds and sharpen its focus on those benefits as it completes the project.

Awhile back, I bumped into someone I had worked with years ago on a product-development initiative, and he mentioned that it was one of the best projects our organization had done. After we parted ways, I tried to reconstruct what was so good about it, because it was not well planned or executed. I realized it was the closeout phase that saved us. In our plan, we had overlooked some business systems that had to be changed to accommodate the new product; we were late getting staff assigned, so we soon fell behind schedule; and we had to replan the project on several occasions as a result of estimating errors and technical problems. Scrambling to recover from the delays, we went over budget by about 10%. In the endgame, however, we made up for those earlier problems by meeting market needs. We made sure that when the product launched, it worked well, it was easy for customers to order and for us to build, and our business systems could support it without difficulty. All that paid off—sales exceeded expectations. That's why stakeholders viewed the project as a success, despite the stumbles in planning and execution.

Once you've achieved your objectives—or determined that they're no longer relevant—you'll take one of three approaches to winding down your project:

The team hands off the project to itself

In such cases, team members become the primary users and maintainers of their own deliverables. When I was at GE, for example, we had a project team that designed and oversaw the installation of a new high-voltage power test facility. Once that was up and running, the head of the team and several other members went on to manage the facility. If your team inherits its own deliverables, it will need to close any administrative accounts or files (such as supplier contracts and purchase orders) associated with development and open new ones for operational deployment.

The team terminates the project

Here, all activities come to a halt, and the organization either releases or redeploys the resources. This can happen when a project has problems, such as a massive overrun, but sometimes it's due to forces outside the team's control. For instance, I once worked with several project teams on coordinating financial processes for two companies planning to merge. The teams had been in place for months and had made great progress when an unexpected government ruling barred the merger at the last minute. The teams disbanded within 24 hours. This type of closeout is administratively straightforward (the end is indisputable, after all), but it can be emotionally difficult because people often lose their assignments—or their jobs—without warning.

The team integrates the project

When using this approach—by far the most common and the most challenging—your team must ensure that others embrace its deliverables and apply them appropriately. In the dozens of new-product initiatives I've helped manage, it has taken as much or more time and work to hand off the product design to the manufacturing and quality organizations and to ensure the training of sales, marketing, and service staff as it has to design, develop, and validate the products themselves. As you integrate your project, you may face organizational resistance to change. If you think that will happen, you can add a transition phase to the project that includes pilot runs, beta tests, and any other activities that will make adoption easier.

Clearly, your closeout method will depend largely on business conditions—and so will the tools and techniques you'll apply within it. Here are a few I've found especially helpful in managing expectations as projects near completion:

The punchlist

This is used mainly in construction projects, but it works well for any type of project where people may try to slide in extra requests—for example, additional features—at the end. The team meets with the stakeholders and reviews the results of project activities. During that review, everyone helps identify remaining tasks, which you put on a "punchlist" of final action items. The team then tackles each item, and when everything on the punchlist is finished, so is the project. Because stakeholders have already agreed on your final to-dos, they'll be much less likely to ask for "just one more thing" at this stage. The punchlist is a good fit when you need to terminate a project, because the team may have a hard time letting go, and this focuses the group on closure. While working with a contract manufacturer of plastic parts several years ago, I helped a team use this tool to ensure that all the tests, inspections, and pilot runs needed to certify a new mold were done and that the mold was brought on line in a timely manner.

The "stakeholder handshake"

Projects that have a fuzzy scope statement—as many research initiatives and small, informal projects do—benefit from this technique because it keeps the work from going too far beyond the plan's boundaries. Meet with your key stakeholders to compare the project's accomplishments with the contract or scope statement, and ask them to agree on whether the project is indeed finished. Have them set an end point or elect to close the project now and, if necessary, open a new one. Such meetings tend to include wide-ranging discussions of options, so it's good to come prepared with several proposals. Following the meeting, document the stakeholders' decision and circulate it so there's no confusion. When I conduct a project-management assessment for an organization, I often close it in this fashion. Many times, I've been asked to "see what we need to improve." After I complete my review, I meet with the executive who hired me. Usually we agree that the assessment is over, discuss the findings, and then determine if I'm needed to help implement them.

The "scope creep parking lot"

During project execution, eager stakeholders may have proposed additional ideas, or team members may have been tempted to add bells and whistles. Ideally, you've captured those items in a list that some project managers call the "scope creep parking lot," so they're not lost—

but they also haven't derailed the plan by introducing new activities or changing boundaries. Now that you're closing the project, it's time to review this list so you can create follow-on proposals for your stakeholders. This technique can be effective when a team prepares to hand off a project to itself because stakeholders may be more likely to accept the deliverables if they know they'll have the opportunity to tweak them later. I've used the scope creep parking lot on several software-development projects. In each case, although minor issues were found during user-acceptance testing, the projects could close because we worked them into the scope for the next release.

Whichever closeout approach and tools you use, don't forget to celebrate your team's achievements. Success breeds success. Even on projects that weren't perfectly planned or executed, team members have worked hard to meet the business objectives and should be rewarded if they've done so. This will encourage them to do good work for you in the future—and the positive example will prompt other teams to achieve their project goals as well. Hold off on discussing opportunities for improvement. It's best to do that in a separate lessons-learned session that's focused on improving the way you manage the next project. For now, take a moment to "bask in the glow" of your current project.

Ray Sheen teaches and consults on project and process management. He has more than 25 years of experience leading projects in defense, product development, manufacturing, IT, and other areas, and has run a project management office in GE's Electrical Distribution business.

Chapter 21
Capturing Lessons Learned

by Ray Sheen

Though every project is different, you can and should always learn from what you've just done. Companies with a project management office (PMO) conduct a **lessons-learned session**—sometimes called a **postmortem** or an **after-action review**—as a formal part of each project's closeout. Those without a PMO typically share insights informally, as team members reminisce. Either way, it's important to capture learning while the experience is still fresh.

For example, I recently led a small project that lasted only a few months, and the team gathered for a dinner immediately after we wrapped things up to talk about what went right and what went wrong. It was a great conversation, and the next project we do will be better because of it. Since the project had a short time frame and the team was intact for the whole thing, it was relatively easy to discuss all aspects, from early planning through completion. When we returned from the dinner, one of the other team members and I updated the project folder with notes about our lessons learned.

By contrast, when I managed an engineering department at a *Fortune* 500 company, some of our projects lasted three years, and the core teams inevitably changed over time. I remember conducting a lessons-learned session with a product development team right after it had launched a new offering. Unfortunately, only one person in the room had been on board back when the project began—and she had moved into a different role by the time it was winding down. With the benefit of hindsight, we could spot errors that the original team had made in the project plan. But we could not identify the events or explain the thinking that led to those errors, since most of us had not been there. From then on, I took a different approach to long-term projects: I started gathering lessons after each phase rather than waiting until the project's end, so the team could clearly recall and accurately analyze what happened. This had the added bonus of allowing us to incorporate the lessons sooner.

When I conduct lessons-learned sessions, I follow a four-step process:

1. Evaluate the business case

The first question I ask is, "Has the project delivered on its promised result?" This isn't meant to help you judge how well the team did the work; it's to gauge whether the project has met senior management's expectations as clarified in the project selection and approval process—and whether those goals were really within reach. Projects are approved on the basis of forecasted business benefits, such as sales growth, cost reduction, cycle-time improvement, defect reduction, or increased capacity. Whatever the forecasted benefit, has it been realized? If not, were the original assumptions and project justifications inaccurate? By carefully examining these issues and sharing the findings with the project's sponsor, a team can improve its organization's ability to select projects and to establish realistic objectives in project charters. If you have a PMO, it will normally take responsibility for incorporating such lessons into project-initiation processes.

2. Evaluate the project plan

Next I ask, "Was the project plan reasonable and appropriate for the project goal and business conditions?" I consider whether it excluded any necessary activities or included any unnecessary ones. I also look at the cost and schedule estimates for each activity. These should reflect the business and technology conditions at the time the project began and provide sensible buffers. Then I review the initial risk assessment to determine which risks were not anticipated, which ones were improperly rated, and which response approaches were inadequate. Finally, I consider the practices established for both team and stakeholder communication. Did the plan allow enough opportunities for updates and information exchange? Did conversations take place at the right times, with the right people? Were decisions made in a timely fashion?

3. Evaluate the project-management methodology

The third question I ask is, "Were the organization's project-management procedures and systems beneficial?" To answer it, I focus on whether the company even *has* procedures, templates, or checklists; how current and relevant they are (if they do exist); how appropriate the mandated reviews and control points were for the project; and how useful the project-management information system was in communicating the project's plans and status to all the players.

Lessons learned are often embodied in companies' project-management procedures and systems. When I served as a consultant to a midsize contract manufacturer, I was surprised to find that it had no centralized project-management procedures, even though all of its work was project based. The firm simply hired experienced project managers and allowed them free rein. This led to a "rock star" mentality among project managers and no consistency in approach. Anyone assigned to a new project team had to learn new scheduling, budgeting, and reporting techniques. The duplication of systems and resulting inefficiency in project execution took a high toll on the organization. Individuals participating on multiple projects had to support multiple, often conflicting, meetings and report formats, leading to numerous "re-dos." The company established a PMO, and over the next three to four months we created the procedures and systems that allowed for coordinated, simplified project planning and execution.

4. Evaluate individuals' performance

Last, I ask, "What feedback do I need to give team members on their performance (good or bad), and what should I tell their supervisors?" I recommend following this step, even if it's not officially required, for all core team members. I typically ask the full team to help identify the "superheroes" among them. This both publicly reinforces the importance of contributing your best and minimizes the impression that the project leader is playing favorites. The members with poor performance I address individually. Of course, specific methods for conducting any performance appraisals must be in accordance with local human resource practices.

An effective lessons-learned process encourages continuous improvement. However, in my experience, the reports from these sessions are seldom read by anyone—so don't pin all your hopes on the documentation you've tucked away in the project file. Instead, turn the lessons into a list of action items for the PMO or for your team members to ensure that they are incorporated into the next project. Apply the insights right away by updating checklists, tweaking review processes, and making any other necessary adjustments before the next project launches.

Ray Sheen teaches and consults on project and process management. He has more than 25 years of experience leading projects in defense, product development, manufacturing, IT, and other areas, and has run a project management office in GE's Electrical Distribution business.

Glossary

Charter. A concise written description of the project's intended work. The charter may contain the name of the sponsor, the project's benefits to the organization, a description of the objectives, the expected time frame, and a budget.

Critical Path Method. A planning technique used for complex projects that consist of several activities. Any activities that need to be completed before others can move forward are considered "critical"—in other words, necessary for the on-time success of the project. The total duration of the project is defined by the critical path.

Gantt chart. A bar chart showing when project tasks should begin and when they should end.

Launch. A special meeting or event that marks a project's official beginning.

Adapted from *Harvard Business Essentials: Managing Projects Large and Small* (product #3213), Harvard Business Review Press, 2004.

Management review. A meeting where stakeholders may examine several projects together, as well as individually, to see if the portfolio as a whole will generate the desired business results and to identify weaknesses.

Network diagram. A scheduling chart that indicates all the relationships between tasks and reveals the critical path. Generally synonymous with a **PERT chart** (below).

Performance Evaluation and Review Technique (PERT). A scheduling method that, when charted, represents every task as a node that connects with other nodes required to complete the project. A **PERT chart** may have many parallel or interconnecting networks of tasks, so periodic reviews are encouraged for complex projects. Unlike the Gantt chart, it indicates all the important task relationships and project milestones.

Post-evaluation. A meeting where the project team debriefs and documents its process for the purpose of learning and sharing lessons and making improvements. Also called a **lessons-learned session,** a **postmortem,** or an **after-action review.**

Project management office. A corporate office (typically in a large company) that establishes processes and templates to guide an organization's project managers in planning and execution, provides assistance to individuals trying to apply those processes, and sometimes manages individual projects.

Project Steering Committee. A group that approves the project charter, secures resources, and adjudicates all requests to change key project elements, including deliverables, the schedule, and the budget.

Punchlist. The project team's final list of action items, approved by key stakeholders.

Scope creep. The tendency (often as a result of pressure from stakeholders) to permit changes that exceed a project's scope and may wreak havoc on the schedule, the quality of the work, or the budget.

Scope creep parking lot. A list of additional ideas or bells and whistles proposed during a project. The idea is to "park" them so they can be revisited later, without danger of derailing the current project.

Stoplight chart. A project-monitoring tool that uses red, yellow, and green color coding to indicate the status of each project activity.

Sunk costs. Project investments that are no longer recoverable.

Technical review. A meeting where an independent team of experts provides an in-depth analysis of project results to ensure that team members did the work accurately, completely, and to the right quality standard. Sometimes called a **peer review.**

Tollgate review. A meeting where the project team summarizes the results of the preceding phase and presents a plan for the next phase so stakeholders can decide whether to approve, redirect, or cancel the project. Also called a **stage-gate review,** or a **phase-gate review.**

Variance. The difference (positive or negative) between actual and expected results in the budget. Managers use variance to spot sources of trouble and areas of exceptional performance.

Work Breakdown Structure (WBS). A planning routine that breaks down a project's goal into the many tasks required to achieve it. The time and money needed to complete those tasks are then estimated.

Index

Notes

Notes

Notes

Notes

Notes

Notes

Notes

Notes

Notes

→ Turn Blank Stares into Standing Ovations

Contrary to common practice, presentations aren't just an opportunity to overwhelm an audience with a sea of bullet points and uninspiring charts. Used properly, presentations can be a powerful tool in your quest to win the hearts and minds of executives, colleagues, customers, and shareholders.

But you won't achieve these results by accident. You need insight, technique, and confidence—exactly what you'll get from the *HBR Guide to Persuasive Presentations Ebook + Video Case Study.*

Purchase of the *HBR Guide to Persuasive Presentations* ebook includes a 20-minute video case study. In the video case study, the CEO of a renewable energy company shows how author Nancy Duarte's smart, practical advice helped him capture the attention of investors, industry experts, and other high-stakes audiences.

THIS ENGAGING 20-MINUTE VIDEO:

→ Illustrates some of the guide's most important points with real-life examples

→ Can be viewed online or offline from any device, at any time, as often as you like

→ Gets you up to speed quickly on key presentation techniques

Order the *HBR Guide to Persuasive Presentations Ebook + Video Case Study* online today.
Available exclusively at hbr.org/store for just $39.95.

Or call 1-800-668-6780. Outside the U.S. and Canada, call +1-617-783-7450. (Product #11150V)

Smart advice and inspiration from a source you trust.

Whether you need help tackling today's most urgent work challenge or shaping your organization's strategy for the future, *Harvard Business Review* has got you covered.

HBR Guides Series

HOW-TO ESSENTIALS FROM LEADING EXPERTS

HBR Guide to Better Business Writing
HBR Guide to Finance Basics for Managers
HBR Guide to Getting the Right Work Done
HBR Guide to Managing Up and Across
HBR Guide to Persuasive Presentations
HBR Guide to Project Management

HBR's 10 Must Reads Series

IF YOU READ NOTHING ELSE, READ THESE DEFINITIVE ARTICLES FROM HARVARD BUSINESS REVIEW

HBR's 10 Must Reads on Change Management
HBR's 10 Must Reads on Leadership
HBR's 10 Must Reads on Managing People
HBR's 10 Must Reads on Managing Yourself
HBR's 10 Must Reads on Strategy
HBR's 10 Must Reads: The Essentials